CROCHET

The Best of
Crochet on the Double™

General Information

Many of the products used in this pattern book can be purchased from local craft, fabric and variety stores, or from the Annie's Attic Needlecraft Catalog (see Customer Service information on page 64).

Contents

General Instructions

Many of the products used in this pattern book can be purchased from local craft, fabric and variety stores or from the Annie's Attic Needlecraft Catalog.

The stitch patterns at the back of the book are ideal for creating everything from sweaters to tissue covers, place mats to afghans. All sizes and weights of yarn can be used with this technique.

Always check your gauge, adjusting hook size and tension as needed. If designing your own project, choose a stitch pattern, and then determine the gauge and hook size needed to create your design. If choosing a pattern in this book, compare your gauge against the gauge given in the pattern instructions.

Double-ended hooks come in a variety of sizes, most commonly D through P, and are manufactured in aluminum, plastic and wood mediums. Try all 3 to determine what feels best; comfort plays an important role in needle arts enjoyment. Hooks with cables are available to help with stitching large projects.

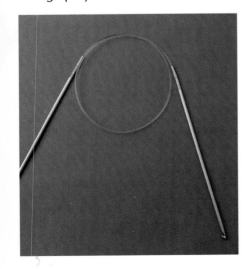

Shown are 3 gauge samples and 3 diverse hook sizes. The same stitch pattern takes on a different texture and look in proportion to the size of the hook used.

G double-ended hook,
2 shells = 1¼ in.; 6 pattern rows = ¼ in

K double-ended hook,
2 shells = 1¾ inches; 4 pattern rows = ¼ inch

P double-ended hook,
2 shells = 2¾ inches; pattern rows = 2 inches

Cotton Fleece yarn is provided by Brown Sheep Company Inc., 100662 County Road 16, Mitchell, NE 69357.

NOTES
When turning the hook at the end of the row, alternate directions. For instance, if you turned the hook to the right at the end of row 1, turn it to the left at the end of row 2. Turning the hook in the same direction each time will tangle the yarn.
Holding the double-ended hook like a knife makes it easier to use.

GENERAL INSTRUCTIONS
Insert hook in 2nd ch from hook, yo and pull through *(see photo A)*, leaving lp on hook. *To **pull up a lp**, insert hook in next ch, yo and pull through; rep from * across *(see photo B)*.

A

B

Each of these lps counts as a stitch and is referred to as a vertical bar.

Leaving all lps on hook, drop color A, turn hook and slide all lps to opposite end of hook *(see photo C)*.

C

To **work lps off hook**, with color B, place slip knot on hook *(see photo D)*.

D

Pull slip knot through first lp on hook *(see photo E)*.

E

Pulling the slip knot through the first lp makes the first st of the row. Yo, pull through next 2 lps on hook (see photo F);

When you pull through the 2 lps in this step, insert hook through 1 lp of each color. The sts you are making in this step are referred to as the Horizontal Bar.

To **work rem lps off hook**, [yo, pull through next 2 lps on hook] across, leaving last lp on hook (see photo G), **do not turn.**

You will now have only 1 lp on your hook. This lp counts as the first vertical bar of the next row. Never turn after working the lps off your hook.

Sk first vertical bar, insert hook under next vertical bar, yo and pull up a lp (see photo H).

Pull up a lp in each vertical bar across, drop color B (see photo I).

If you have trouble keeping the lps on the hook, cap the unused end with a rubber knit stopper or a piece of cork. Turn and slide all lps to opposite end of hook (see photo J).

Pick up color A from row below, yo and pull through first lp on hook (see photo K).

This is the same process as in step E, except you are using the yarn from the row below rather than placing a slip knot on the hook.

Yo, pull through next 2 lps on hook (see photo L).

Remember to Insert hook through 1 lp of each color when working the lps off in this step.

To **work rem lps off hook**, [yo and pull through next 2 lps on hook] across, leaving last lp on hook, **do not turn** (see photo M).

Sk first vertical bar, pull up lp in next vertical bar (see photo N), pull up lp in each bar across, drop color A, turn. Slide all lps to opposite end of hook.

Continue alternating colors until ending with color A (or color specified in individual pattern instructions).

Sk first vertical bar, sl st (or use the stitch called for in the individual pattern instructions) across (see photo O). Fasten off. ❑❑

Basic Panels

Design by Jennifer McClain

SKILL LEVEL

INTERMEDIATE

FINISHED SIZE
10 x 10½ inches

MATERIALS
- ❏ Medium (worsted) weight cotton yarn: 1 oz/50 yds/28g each pale yellow and variegated
- ❏ Size H/8/5mm double-ended crochet hook or size needed to obtain gauge
- ❏ Size G/6/4mm crochet hook or size needed to obtain gauge
- ❏ Tapestry needle

GAUGE
Double-ended hook: 3 sts = 1 inch; 7 pattern rows = 1 inch
Size G hook: 7 sts = 2 inches

PATTERN NOTE
Read General Instructions on pages 3–5 before beginning pattern.

INSTRUCTIONS
Strip
Make 3.
Row 1: With double-ended hook and pale yellow, ch 10, pull up lp in 2nd

ch from hook, pull up lp in each ch across, turn. *(10 lps on hook).*
Row 2: With variegated, work lps off hook, **do not turn.**
Row 3: Sk first vertical bar, pull up lp in next vertical bar and in each bar across, turn.
Row 4: With pale yellow, work lps off hook, do not turn.
Row 5: Sk first vertical bar, pull up lp in each vertical bar across, turn.
Rows 6–68: Rep rows 2–5 consecutively, ending with row 4.

Row 69: Ch 1, sk first vertical bar, sl st in each vertical bar across, fasten off.

Edging
Working around outer edge in sts and in ends of rows, with size G hook, join pale yellow with sc in any corner st, 2 sc in same st, evenly spacing sts so piece lies flat, sc around with 3 sc in each corner st, join with sl st in beg sc. Fasten off.
Sew long edges of Strips tog to form dishcloth. ❏❏

Sunny Scallops

Design by Mary Ann Sipes

SKILL LEVEL

INTERMEDIATE

FINISHED SIZE
33 x 47 inches

MATERIALS
- ❑ Fine (sport) weight yarn:
    14 oz/1,260 yds/397g yellow
    7 oz/630 yds/199g white
- ❑ Size G/6/4mm double-ended swivel crochet hook or size needed to obtain gauge
- ❑ Size F/5/3.75mm hook

FINE

GAUGE
With double-ended hook: 4 sts = 1 inch; 4 pattern rows = 1 inch

PATTERN NOTES
Read General Instructions on pages 3–5 before beginning pattern.
Use double-ended hook unless otherwise stated.

SPECIAL STITCHES
Single crochet loop (sc lp): Insert hook in next st, yo, pull lp through, ch 1.
Double crochet loop (dc lp): Yo, insert hook in next st, yo, pull lp through, yo, pull through 2 lps on hook.
Scallop: 5 dc lps under next horizontal bar.

INSTRUCTIONS
AFGHAN
Row 1: With yellow, ch 120, pull up lp in 2nd ch from hook, pull up lp in each ch across, turn. *(120 lps on hook)*
Row 2: With white, work lps off hook, **do not turn.**
Row 3: Ch 1, sk first vertical bar, **sc lp** *(see Special Stitches)* under each **horizontal bar** *(see illustration)* across, turn.

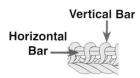

Vertical Bar

Horizontal Bar →

Row 4: With yellow, work lps off hook, do not turn.
Row 5: Ch 2 *(counts as first dc lp)*, **dc lp** *(see Special Stitches)* in first vertical bar, sk next 4 horizontal bars, [**scallop** —see Special Stitches, under next horizontal bar, sk next 4 horizontal bars] across to last vertical bar, 2 dc lps in last vertical bar, turn. *(23 scallops, 4 dc lps)*
Row 6: With white, work lps off hook, do not turn.
Row 7: Ch 1, sk first vertical bar, sc lp under each horizontal bar across to last vertical bar, sc lp in last vertical bar, turn.
Rows 8–176: Rep rows 4-7 consecutively, ending with row 4.

Row 177: Ch 1, sk first vertical bar, sl st in each vertical bar across. Fasten off.

BORDER
Rnd 1: Working around outer edge, with size F hook, join yellow with sl st in first st of last row, ch 3 *(counts as first dc)*, 8 dc in same st, *sk next st, sc in next st, sk next 2 sts, [5 dc in next st, sk next 2 sts, sc in next st, sk next 2 sts] across to last st, 9 dc in last st, working in ends of rows, sk next white row, sc in next yellow row, sk next white row, [5 dc in next yellow row, sk next white row, sc in next yellow row, sk next white row] across*, working in starting ch on opposite side of row 1, 9 dc in first ch, rep between *, join with sl st in 3rd ch of beg ch-3. Fasten off.
Rnd 2: With size F hook, join white with sc in 3rd st of first 9-dc corner, *[ch 2, sk next st, sc in next st] twice, (dc, ch 2, dc) in next sc, [sc in center st of next 5-dc group, (dc, ch 2, dc) in next sc] across** to next 9-dc corner, sc in 3rd st of next 9-dc corner, rep from * around, ending last rep at **, join with sl st in beg sc. Fasten off.
Rnd 3: With size F hook, join yellow with sl st in first sc, (ch 3, 4 dc) in same st, sc in next ch sp, skipping all dc [5 dc in next sc, sc in next ch sp] around, join with sl st in 3rd ch of beg ch-3. Fasten off. ❑❑

Designs by Debbie Tabor

FINISHED SIZES
Square Block: 3 inches square
Triangle Block: 3 inches tall
Round Block: 2½ inches tall x 3½ inches wide.

MATERIALS FOR 1 OF EACH
❑ Medium (worsted) weight yarn: 1½ oz/75 yds/ 43g each lime, yellow, blue, teal, bright pink and dark pink
❑ Size G/6/4mm double-ended crochet hook or size needed to obtain gauge
❑ Tapestry needle
❑ Polyester fiberfill

GAUGE
5 sts = 1 inch; 10 rows = 1 inch

PATTERN NOTE
Read General Instructions on pages 3–5 before beginning pattern.

INSTRUCTIONS

SQUARE BLOCK
Side
Make 6.
Row 1: With bright pink, ch 15, pull up lp in 2nd ch from hook, pull up lp in each ch across, turn. *(15 lps on hook)*
Row 2: With dark pink, work lps off hook, **do not turn.**
Row 3: Ch 1, sk first vertical bar, pull

up lp in top strand of each horizontal bar across *(see illustration)*, turn.

Vertical Bar
Horizontal Bar

Row 4: With bright pink, work lps off hook, do not turn.
Row 5: Ch 1, sk first vertical bar, pull up lp in top strand of each horizontal bar across, turn.
Rows 6–28: Rep rows 2–5 consecutively, ending with row 4. At end of last row, fasten off.
Sew pieces tog forming a square, stuffing before closing.

TRIANGLE BLOCK
Side
Make 3.
Row 1: With blue, ch 15, pull up lp in 2nd ch from hook, pull up lp in each ch across, turn. *(15 lps on hook)*
Row 2: With teal, work lps off hook, do not turn.
Row 3: Ch 1, sk first vertical bar, pull up lp in top strand of each horizontal bar across, turn.
Row 4: With blue, work lps off hook, do not turn.
Row 5: Ch 1, sk first vertical bar, sl st in top strand of next horizontal bar, pull up lp in top strand of each horizontal bar across to last horizontal bar, sl st in top strand of last horizontal bar, turn. *(13 lps on hook)*
Rows 6–28: Rep rows 2–5 consecutively, ending with row 4 and 3 lps on hook.

Row 29: Ch 1, sl st in top strand of each horizontal bar across. Fasten off.
Sew ends of rows of 3 Sides tog leaving bottom open.

Base
Row 1: With blue, ch 15, pull up lp in 2nd ch from hook, pull up lp in each ch across, turn. *(15 lps on hook)*
Row 2: With teal, work lps off hook, do not turn.
Row 3: Ch 1, sk first vertical bar, sl st in top strand of next horizontal bar, pull up lp in top strand of each horizontal bar across to last horizontal bar, sl st in top strand of last horizontal bar, turn. *(13 lps on hook)*
Row 4: With blue, work lps off hook, do not turn.
Row 5: Ch 1, sk first vertical bar, sl st in top strand of next horizontal bar, pull up lp in top strand of each horizontal bar across to last horizontal bar, sl st in top strand of last horizontal bar, turn. *(11 lps on hook)*
Rows 6–14: Rep rows 2–5 consecutively, ending with row 2 and 3 lps on hook.
Row 15: Ch 1, sl st in top strand of each horizontal bar across. Fasten off.
Easing to fit, sew Base to bottom of Sides, stuffing before closing.

ROUND BLOCK
Top/Bottom Piece
Make 2.
Row 1: With yellow, ch 8, pull up lp in 2nd ch from hook, pull up lp in each ch across, turn. *(8 lps on hook)*
Row 2: With lime, work lps off hook, do not turn.
Row 3: Ch 1, sk first vertical bar, pull

up lp in top strand of each horizontal bar across, turn.

Row 4: With yellow, work lps off hook, do not turn.

Row 5: Ch 1, sk first vertical bar, pull up lp in top strand of each horizontal bar across, turn.

Rows 6–84: Rep rows 2–5 consecutively, ending with row 4.

Row 85: Ch 1, sk first vertical bar, sl st in top strand of each horizontal bar across. Fasten off.

With tapestry needle, weave yellow through ends of rows on 1 side, pull tight to gather into a circle, secure. Matching sts, sew first and last rows tog.

Side
Row 1: With yellow, ch 12, pull up lp in 2nd ch from hook, pull up lp in each ch across, turn. *(12 lps on hook)*

Row 2: With lime, work lps off hook, do not turn.

Row 3: Ch 1, sk first vertical bar, pull up lp in top strand of each horizontal bar across, turn.

Row 4: With yellow, work lps off hook, do not turn.

Row 5: Ch 1, sk first vertical bar, pull up lp in top strand of each horizontal bar across, turn.

Rows 6–112: Rep rows 2–5 consecutively, ending with row 4.

Row 113: Ch 1, sk first vertical bar, sl st in top strand of each horizontal bar across. Leaving long end for sewing, fasten off.

Matching sts, sew first and last rows tog. Easing to fit and matching row colors, sew Top and Bottom to Side, stuffing before closing. ❑❑

ABC Blocks

Design by Jessica Gardner

SKILL LEVEL
■■■□
EXPERIENCED

FINISHED SIZE
30 x 33 inches, not including Ruffle

MATERIALS

❑ Medium (worsted) weight yarn:
  16 oz/800 yds/454g white
  8 oz/400 yds/227g each pink, yellow and turquoise
❑ Size H/8/5mm double-ended crochet hook or size needed to obtain gauge
❑ Size H/8/5mm crochet hook
❑ Tapestry needle

GAUGE
Double-ended hook: 8 sts = 2 inches
Each Motif is 10 inches wide x 11 inches long

PATTERN NOTES
See General Instructions on pages 3–5 before beginning pattern.

When picking up loop on horizontal bar, insert hook under **top strand** only *(see illustration).*

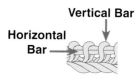

Vertical Bar
Horizontal Bar

SPECIAL STITCH
Puff stitch (puff st): Yo, pull up lp in corresponding opposite-colored vertical bar 4 rows below, [yo, pull up lp in same bar 4 rows below] twice, yo, pull through 7 lps on hook, ch 1 to close, sk 1 lp on last row behind puff st. When working puff st into previous puff st, insert hook under vertical bar formed by ch-1 at top of puff st.

INSTRUCTIONS

WAVES MOTIF
Make 4.

Row 1: With double-ended hook and pink, ch 38 loosely, pull up lp in 2nd ch from hook, pull up lp in each ch across, turn. Fasten off *(38 lps on hook)*

Row 2: With yellow, work lps off hook, **do not turn.**

Row 3: With yellow, ch 1, pull up lp in each of first 2 **horizontal bars** *(see Pattern Notes)*, sk next vertical bar, pull up lp in each of next 2 vertical bars, *pull up lp in each of next 2 horizontal bars, sk next vertical bar, [yo, insert hook in next vertical bar, yo, pull through 2 lps on hook] 4 times, pull up lp in each of next 2 horizontal bars, sk next vertical bar, pull up lp in each of next 2 vertical bars, rep from * twice, pull up lp in each of last 3 horizontal bars, turn.

Row 4: With turquoise, work lps off hook, do not turn.

Row 5: With turquoise, ch 1, pull up lp in first horizontal bar, sk next vertical bar, [yo, insert hook in next vertical bar, yo, pull through 2 lps on hook] 4 times, pull up lp in next 2 horizontal bars, *sk next vertical bar, pull up lp in each of next 2 vertical bars, pull up lp in each of next 2 horizontal bars, sk next vertical bar, [yo, insert hook in next vertical bar, yo, pull through 2 lps on hook] 4 times, pull up lp in each of next 2 horizontal bars, rep from * twice, turn. Fasten off.

Rows 6 & 7: With pink, rep rows 2 and 3.

Rows 8 & 9: With yellow, rep rows 4 and 5.

Rows 10 & 11: With turquoise, rep rows 2 and 3.

Rows 12 & 13: With pink, rep rows 4 and 5.

Rows 14–60: Working color sequence as established in rows 2–13, rep rows 2–5 consecutively, ending with row 4.

Row 61: Continuing in color sequence as established, ch 1, sl st in each horizontal bar across. Fasten off.

WHITE MOTIF
Make 2.

Rows 1–61: Using 2 skeins white yarn and carrying dropped yarn along ends of rows without cutting, rep rows 1–61 of Waves Motif.

A-1 MOTIF
Row 1: With double-ended hook and

pink, ch 39 loosely, pull up lp in 2nd ch from hook, pull up lp in each ch across, turn. *(39 lps on hook)*

Row 2: With white, work lps off hook, do not turn.

Row 3: With white, ch 1, pull up lp in each horizontal bar across, turn.

Row 4: With pink, work lps off hook, do not turn.

Row 5: With pink, ch 1, pull up lp in each horizontal bar across, turn.

Rows 6–12: Rep rows 2–12 once, then rep rows 2–4.

Row 13: To position beg of letter "A," with pink, ch 1, pull up lp in each of first 6 horizontal bars *(7 lps on hook)*, ***puff st** *(see Special Stitch)*, pull up lp in next horizontal bar on last row, puff st*, pull up lp in each of next 21 horizontal bars, rep between *, pull up lp in each of last 6 horizontal bars, turn. Fasten off. *(39 lps on hook)*

Row 14: With pink, work lps off hook.

Row 15: To position beg of number "1" with white, ch 1, pull up lp in each of first 18 horizontal bars *(19 lps on hook)*, puff st, pull up lp in next horizontal bar, puff st, pull up lp in each of last 18 horizontal bars, turn, Fasten off.

Rows 16–63: Rep rows 2–5 consecutively as follows:
Work pink puff sts over rows 16–61 according to Letter A graph;
Work white puff sts over rows 16–63 according to Number "1" graph.

Rows 64–68: Rep rows 2–5 once, then rep row 2.

Row 69: With pink, ch 1, sl st in each horizontal bar across. Fasten off.

B-2 MOTIF

Rows 1–10: Using yellow instead of pink, rep rows 1–10 of A-1 Motif.

Row 11: To position beg of number "2," with white, ch 1, sk first horizontal bar, pull up lp in next 7 horizontal bars *(8 lps on hook)*, puff st, [pull up lp in next horizontal bar, puff st] 11 times, pull up lp in each of last 8 horizontal bars, turn. Fasten off.

Row 12: With yellow, work lps off hook, do not turn.

Row 13: To position beg of letter "B" with yellow, ch 1, sk first horizontal bar, pull up lp in each of next 9 horizontal bars *(10 lps on hook)*, puff st, [pull up lp in next horizontal bar, puff st] 11 times, pull up lp in each of last 6 horizontal bars, turn. Fasten off.

Row 14: With white, work lps off hook, do not turn.

Row 15: Work according to row 15 of Letter "B" graph, ch 1, pull up lp in each horizontal bar across, turn.

Rows 16–63: Rep rows 2–5 consecutively as follows:
Work yellow puff sts over rows 16–61 according to Letter "B" graph;
Work white puff sts over rows 16–63 according to Number "2" graph.

Rows 64–68: Rep rows 2–5 once, then rep row 2.

Row 69: With yellow, ch 1, sl st in each horizontal bar across. Fasten off.

C-3 MOTIF

Rows 1–10: Using turquoise instead of pink, rep rows 1–10 of A-1 Motif.

Row 11: To position beg of number "3" with white, ch 1, sk first horizontal bar, pull up lp in each of next 15 horizontal bars *(16 lps on hook)*, puff st, [pull up lp in next horizontal bar, puff st] 4 times, pull up lp in each of last 14 horizontal bars, turn. Fasten off.

Row 12: With turquoise, work lps off hook, do not turn.

Row 13: To position beg of letter "C" with turquoise, ch 1, sk first horizontal bar, pull up lp in each of next 12 horizontal bars *(13 lps on hook)*, puff st, [pull up lp in next horizontal bar, puff st] 6 times, pull up lp in each of last 13 horizontal bars, turn. Fasten off.

Rows 14–63: Rep rows 2–5 consecutively as follows:

Work turquoise puff sts over rows 14–61 according to Letter "C" graph;

Work white puff sts over rows 14–63 according to Number "3" graph.

Rows 64–68: Rep rows 2–5 consecutively, ending with row 2.

Row 69: With turquoise, ch 1, sl st in each horizontal bar across. Fasten off.

ASSEMBLY

1. Lay Motifs flat as shown in Assembly Diagram.
2. For first vertical seam, using crochet hook, join white with sc at corner

First Square, "A" Side
Work pink puff sts on odd-numbered pink rows (with white side of work facing).

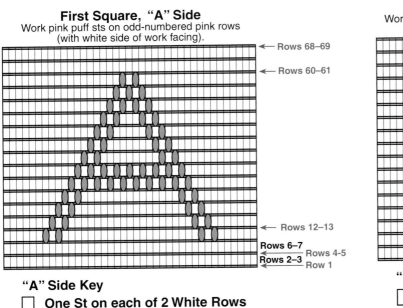

← Rows 68–69
← Rows 60–61
← Rows 12–13
← Rows 6–7
← Rows 4-5
← Rows 2–3
← Row 1

"A" Side Key
☐ One St on each of 2 White Rows
▬ One St on each of 2 Pink Rows
⬭ Pink Puff St

Second Square, "B" Side
Work yellow puff sts on odd-numbered yellow rows (with white side of work facing).

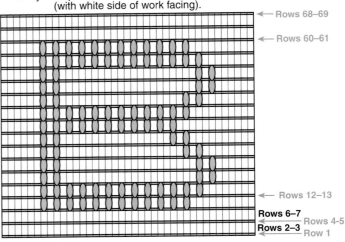

← Rows 68–69
← Rows 60–61
← Rows 12–13
← Rows 6–7
← Rows 4-5
← Rows 2–3
← Row 1

"B" Side Key
☐ One St on each of 2 White Rows
▬ One St on each of 2 Yellow Rows
⬭ Yellow Puff St

First Square, "1" Side
Work white puff sts on odd-numbered white rows (with pink side of work facing).

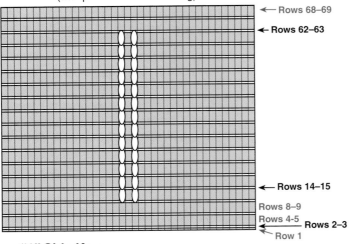

← Rows 68–69
← Rows 62–63
← Rows 14–15
← Rows 8–9
← Rows 4-5
← Rows 2–3
← Row 1

"1" Side Key
▬ One St on each of 2 Pink Rows
☐ One St on each of 2 White Rows
◯ White Puff St

Second Square, "2" Side
Work white puff sts on odd-numbered white rows (with yellow side of work facing).

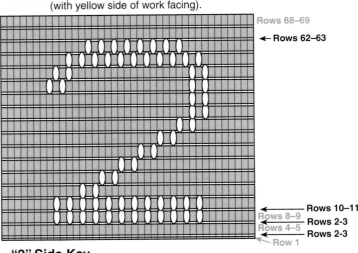

← Rows 68–69
← Rows 62–63
← Rows 10–11
← Rows 8–9
← Rows 2-3
← Rows 4–5
← Rows 2–3
← Row 1

"2" Side Key
▬ One St on each of 2 Yellow Rows
☐ One St on each of 2 White Rows
◯ White Puff St

of 1 Motif (see red X on Assembly Diagram), sc edges of 2 Motifs tog across all 3 pairs of Motifs. Fasten off at red dot on Diagram. Rep for 2nd vertical seam.

3. For horizontal seams, turn Motifs to side and rep step 2.

RUFFLE

Rnd 1: Join white with sl st in corner of assembled Afghan (see black arrow on Assembly Diagram), ch 3 (counts as first dc), dc in same corner, evenly sp 41 dc in ends of rows across each Motif on long edges (total of 123 dc in ends of rows across long edge) and dc in each st or ch across each short edge (total of 115 dc in sts across short edge) with (2 dc, ch 2, 2 dc) in each corner, ending with 2 dc in same corner as joining, ch 2, join with sl st in 3rd ch of beg ch-3, **turn.** Fasten off. (127 dc on each long edge, 119 dc on each short edge, 4 ch sps made)

Rnd 2: With WS of last rnd facing, join pink with sl st in any corner ch sp, ch 5, dc in same ch sp, dc in next dc, [2 dc in next dc, dc in next dc] across to next corner ch sp, *(dc, ch 2, dc) in ch sp, dc in next dc, [2 dc in next dc, dc in next dc] across to next corner ch sp, rep from * twice, join with sl st in 3rd ch of ch-5, turn. Fasten off. (192 dc on each long edge, 180 dc on each short edge, 4 corner ch sps)

Rnd 3: With WS of last rnd facing, join yellow with sl st in any corner ch sp, ch 5, dc in same ch sp, [2 dc in next dc, dc in next dc] across to next corner ch sp, *(dc, ch 2, dc) in ch sp, [dc in next dc, 2 dc in next

dc] across to next corner ch sp, rep from * twice, join with sl st in 3rd ch of beg ch-5, turn. Fasten off. (290 dc on each long edge, 272 dc on each short edge, 4 corner ch sps)

Rnd 4: With WS of last rnd facing, join turquoise with sl st in any corner ch sp, ch 5, dc in same ch sp, 2 dc in next dc, dc in each dc across to 1 dc before next corner ch sp, 2 dc in next dc, *(dc, ch 2, dc) in ch sp,

2 dc in next dc, dc in each dc across to 1 dc before next corner ch sp, 2 dc in next dc, rep from * twice, join with sl st in 3rd ch of beg ch-5, turn. Fasten off.

Rnd 5: With WS of last rnd facing, join white with sc in any corner ch sp, (ch 2, sc, ch 2) in same ch sp, (sc, ch 2) in each st around with (sc, ch 2) twice in each corner ch sp, join with sl st in beg sc. Fasten off. ❑❑

Third Square, "C" Side
Work turquoise puff sts on odd-numbered turquoise rows
(with white side of work facing).

← Rows 68–69
← Rows 60–61
← Rows 12–13
Rows 6–7
Rows 4-5
Rows 2–3
Row 1

"B" Side Key

☐ One St on each of 2 White Rows

▥ One St on each of 2 Turquoise Rows

⬭ Turquoise Puff St

Third Square, "3" Side
Work white puff sts on odd-numbered white rows
(with turquoise side of work facing).

Rows 68–69
← Rows 62–63
← Rows 10–11
Rows 6–7
Rows 4–5
Rows 2–3
Row 1

"3" Side Key

▩ One St on each of 2 Turquoise Rows

☐ One St on each of 2 White Rows

◯ White Puff St

Assembly Diagram

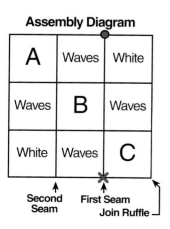

A	Waves	White
Waves	B	Waves
White	Waves	C

Second Seam ↑   First Seam / Join Ruffle ⌐

Faux Monks Cloth

Design by Eleanor Miles-Bradley

FINISHED SIZE
33 x 39 inches

MATERIALS
- ❑ Fine (sport) weight yarn: 25 oz/2,250 yds/ 709g white
- ❑ Medium (worsted) weight yarn: 3 oz/150 yds/85g each variegated blues and variegated browns
- ❑ Size H/8/5mm double-ended swivel crochet hook or size needed to obtain gauge
- ❑ Size F/5/3.75mm crochet hook or size needed to obtain gauge
- ❑ 2 tapestry needles

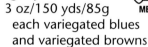

GAUGE
Size H hook and sport yarn: 11 sts = 2 inches, 11 rows = 2 inches
Size F hook and sport yarn: 11 sc = 2 inches

PATTERN NOTE
Read General Instructions on pages 3–5 before beginning pattern.

INSTRUCTIONS
AFGHAN
Row 1: With size H hook and white, ch 181 loosely, pull up lp in 2nd ch from hook, pull up lp in each ch across, turn. *(181 lps on hook)*
Row 2: With separate skein white, work lps off hook, **do not turn.**
Row 3: Ch 1, sk first vertical bar, pull up lp in each vertical bar across, turn.
Row 4: Work lps off hook, do not turn.
Next rows: As you work, 4 rows appear to be 1 ridge and 1 valley, rep rows 3 and 4 alternately until you have 81 ridges on each side, ending with row 4. At end of last row, fasten off.

WEAVE BLUE SIDE
Weave steps 1–3 for each of 7 columns of diamonds:

1. For first section of weaving in each column of diamonds *(indicated by lighter shade of purple on Blues graph)*, cut 4-yd length of variegated blue yarn and thread tapestry needle onto each end of strand. When weaving, take care that this color of yarn does not show on opposite side of work.
2. To begin, run 1 end through st on 2nd ridge of center where indicated on Blues graph and pull to center of strand. Weave each end of strand according to Blues graph, secure ends of strand and run back through weaving yarn to hide. *(If desired, loose ends can be stitched in place on weaving yarn using sewing needle and matching-color sewing thread.)*
3. Using another 4-yd length of variegated blue yarn, weave rem of same column as indicated by darker shade of purple on Blues graph.

WEAVE BROWN SIDE
1. For each straight line of weaving on narrow columns only *(pink weaving lines on Browns graph)*, cut 2-yd length of variegated brown yarn and thread tapestry needle onto 1 end. Weave strand according to straight stitching lines on Browns graph, secure both ends of strand *(see pink dots on graph)* and run back through weaving yarn to hide *(if desired, loose ends can be stitched to weaving yarn using sewing needle and matching-color sewing thread)*.
2. For each rem section of weaving in wide or narrow columns *(one half of strand indicated by light brown and other half of strand by dark brown on Browns graph)*, cut 4-yd length of variegated brown yarn and thread a tapestry needle onto each end of strand. Run 1 end through st on first ridge of center

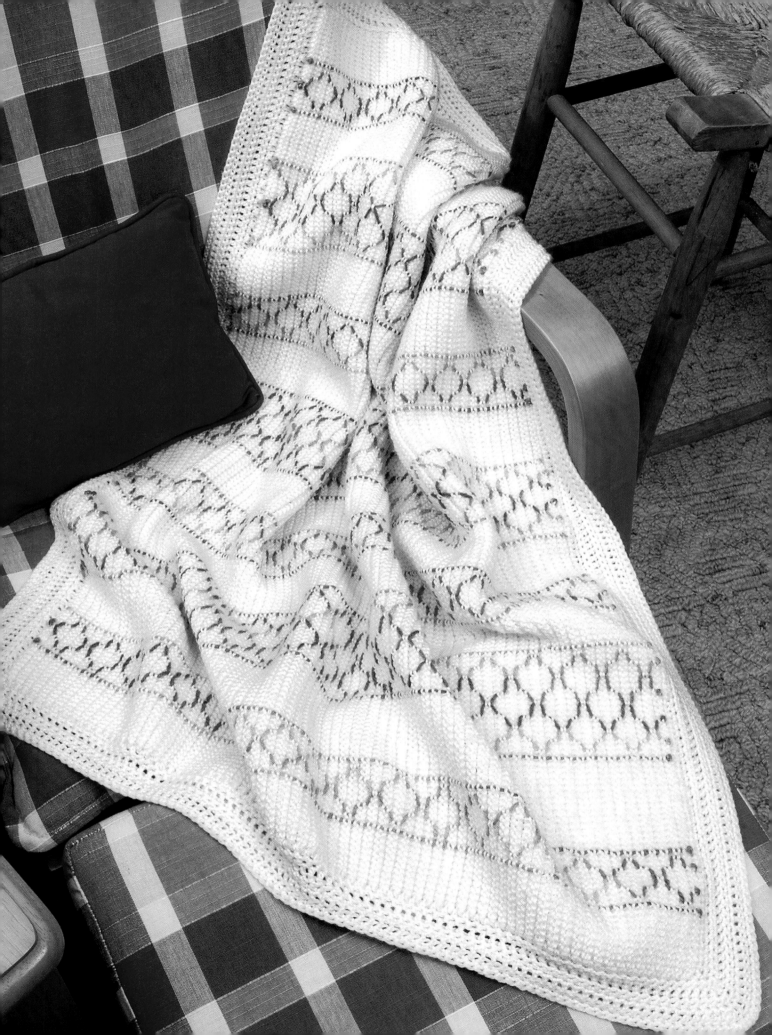

(see graph) and pull to center of strand. Weave each half of strand according to graph, secure and hide ends of strand in same manner.

BORDER

Rnd 1: Using size F hook, join white with sc in last st at any corner, 2 sc in same st, sp sts evenly so edges lie flat, sc in sts and in ends of rows around with 3 sc in each corner st, join with sl st in beg sc, turn.

Rnd 2: Ch 1, sc in each st around with 3 sc in each center corner st, join with sl st in beg sc, turn.

Rnd 3: Ch 3 (counts as first dc), dc in each st around with 3 dc in each center corner st, join with sl st in 3rd ch of beg ch-3, turn.

Rnds 4 & 5: Ch 1, sc in each st around with 3 sc in each center corner st, join with sl st in beg sc, turn.

Rnds 6–8: Rep rnds 3–5. At end of last rnd, fasten off. ❑❑

Blues
Go **over valleys** where weave stitches are shown; go **under two strands on ridges** where weave stitches are not shown.

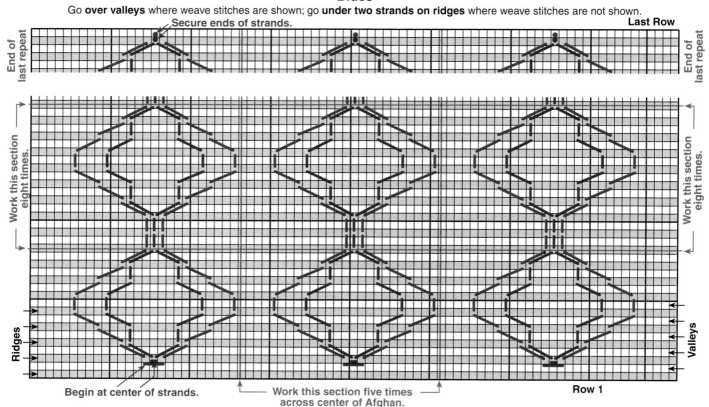

Browns
Go **over valleys** where stitches are shown; go **under two strands on ridges** where stitches are not shown.

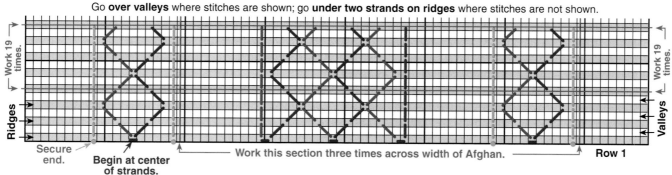

Diagonal Squares

Design by Anne Halliday

SKILL LEVEL

INTERMEDIATE

FINISHED SIZE

48 x 63 inches

MATERIALS

- ❏ Red Heart Super Saver medium (worsted) weight yarn (7 oz/364 yds/ 198g per skein):
    - 4 skeins #382 country blue
    - 2 skeins each #313 Aran and #320 cornmeal
- ❏ Size I/9/5.5mm double-ended crochet hook or size needed to obtain gauge
- ❏ Size I/9/5.5mm crochet hook or size needed to obtain gauge
- ❏ Tapestry needle
- ❏ Stitch markers

GAUGE

Double-ended hook: 7 sts = 2 inches; 9 pattern rows = 1 inch
Size I hook: each Triangle is 4 x 8 inches
Each Block measures 5 inches across including Edging.

PATTERN NOTE

Read General Instructions on pages 3–5 before beginning pattern.

INSTRUCTIONS

AFGHAN

Block
Make 83.

Row 1: With double-ended hook and Aran, ch 11, pull up lp in 2nd ch from hook and in each ch across, turn. *(11 lps on hook)*

Row 2: With cornmeal, work lps off hook, **do not turn.** Predominantly cornmeal side of Block will be RS of work.

Row 3: Sk first vertical bar, pull up lp in each vertical bar across, turn.

Row 4: With Aran, work lps off hook, do not turn.

Row 5: Sk first vertical bar, pull up lp in each vertical bar across, turn.

Rows 6–24: Rep rows 2–5 consecutively, ending with row 4.

Row 25: Ch 1, sk first vertical bar, sl st in each vertical bar across. Fasten off both colors.

Edging

Rnd 1: Working around entire outer edge with RS facing, with crochet hook and country blue, join with sl st in 2nd st of last row, sl st in each of next 8 sts, ch 1, sk last st, *evenly sp 9 sl sts across ends of rows, ch 1*, working in starting ch on opposite side of row 1, sk first ch, sl st in each of next 9 chs, ch 1, sk last ch, rep between *, join with sl st in beg sl st. *(9 sts across each side between corner chs)*

Rnd 2: Working this rnd in **back lps** only *(see Stitch Guide)*, ch 1, sc in each of first 9 sts, ch 1, dc in next corner ch, ch 1, *sc in each of next 9 sts, ch 1, dc in next corner ch, ch 1, rep from * around, join with sl st in beg sc. Fasten off.

Rnd 3: Join Aran with sc in first ch sp after any corner dc, *sc in each of next 2 sts, ch 1, sk next st, sc in each of next 3 sts, ch 1, sk next st, sc in each of next 2 sts, sc in next ch sp, ch 3, sk next corner dc**, sc in next ch sp, rep from * around, ending last rep at **, join with sl st in beg sc. Fasten off.

Rnd 4: Join country blue with sl st in any corner ch sp, ch 3 *(counts as first dc)*, (2 dc, ch 3, 3 dc) in same ch sp, ch 1, [3 dc in next ch sp, ch 1] twice, *(3 dc, ch 3, 3 dc) in next corner ch sp, ch 1, [3 dc in next ch sp, ch 1] twice, rep from * around, join with sl st in 3rd ch of beg ch-3. Fasten off.

Holding Blocks WS tog, matching sts, with country blue, sew tog according to illustration.

TRIANGLE
Make 24.

Row 1 (WS): With country blue, ch 6, (3 dc, ch 3, 3 dc, ch 1, tr) in 6th ch from hook, turn. *(6 dc, 2 tr, 2 ch-1 sps, 1 ch-3 sp)*

Row 2: Ch 5 *(counts as first tr and ch-1 sp)*, 3 dc in next ch sp, ch 1, (3 dc, ch 3, 3 dc) in next ch sp, ch 1, 3 dc in next ch sp, ch 1, tr in 4th ch of ch-5, turn.

Row 3: Ch 5, [3 dc in next ch sp, ch 1] twice, (3 dc, ch 3, 3 dc) in next ch sp, ch 1, [3 dc in next ch sp, ch 1] twice, tr in 4th ch of ch-5, turn.

Row 4: Ch 5, [3 dc in next ch sp, ch 1] 3 times, (3 dc, ch 3, 3 dc) in next ch sp, ch 1, [3 dc in next ch sp, ch 1] 3 times, tr in 4th ch of ch-5. Fasten off.

Holding WS tog, matching sts, with country blue, sew Triangles into indentations between Blocks.

BORDER

Rnd 1: Working around entire outer edge, with crochet hook and country blue, join with sc in first ch sp after seam on corner Block according to diagram, ◊ch 1, sc in center st of next 3-dc group, ch 1, [sc in next ch sp, ch 1, sc in center st of next 3-dc group, ch 1] 3 times, sc in next ch sp, ch 2 *(mark as corner ch sp)*, sk next seam, working in ends of rows on Triangles, [sc in next row, ch 1, *(sc, ch 1) twice in next row, sc in next row, ch 1, {(sc, ch 1) 2 times) in next row*, sk ch on opposite side of row 1, rep between *, sc in next row, ch 1, sk next seam] across to next corner Block, ch 2 *(mark as comer ch sp)*, sk next seam◊◊, working across corner Block, sc in next ch sp, rep from ◊ around, ending last rep at ◊◊, join with sl st in beg sc.

Rnds 2–4: Sl st in first ch sp, ch 1, sc in same ch sp, ch 1, *[sc in next ch sp, ch 1] around with (sc, ch 1) twice in each corner ch sp, join with sl st in beg sc. At end of last rnd, fasten off. ❏❏

Join rnd 1 of Border here.

Diagonal Squares Assembly Illustration

`✎` = Triangle placement

Easter Afghan

Design by Anne Halliday

SKILL LEVEL

INTERMEDIATE

FINISHED SIZE
48½ x 68½ inches

MATERIALS
- ❑ Red Heart Super Saver worsted yarn (7 oz/ 364 yds/198g per skein):
  5 skeins #313 Aran
  3 skeins each #372 rose pink and #631 light sage
- ❑ Size I/9/5.5mm double-ended crochet hook or size needed to obtain gauge
- ❑ Size I/9/5.5mm crochet hook or size needed to obtain gauge
- ❑ Tapestry needle

GAUGE
Double-ended hook: 4 sts = 1 inch; 8 pattern rows = 1 inch
Crochet hook: Rnd 1 of Block C = 1¾ inches across.
Each Block A and Block B = 5 inches square with Edging.
Each Block C and Block D = 5 inches square.

PATTERN NOTE
Read General Instructions on pages 3–5 before beginning pattern.

SPECIAL STITCH
Horizontal cluster (horizontal cl): Ch 3, yo, insert hook in 3rd ch from hook, yo, pull lp through, yo, pull through 2 lps on hook, yo, insert hook in same ch, yo, pull lp through, yo, pull through 2 lps on hook, yo, pull through all lps on hook.

INSTRUCTIONS
AFGHAN
Block A
Make 28.
Row 1: With double-ended hook and Aran, ch 13, pull up lp in 2nd ch from hook and in each ch across, turn. *(13 lps on hook)*

Row 2: With rose pink, work lps off hook, do not turn. Predominantly rose pink side of Block will be RS of work.

Row 3: Sk first vertical bar, pull up lp in each vertical bar across, turn.

Row 4: With Aran, work lps off hook, **do not turn.**

Row 5: Sk first vertical bar, pull up lp in each vertical bar across, turn.

Rows 6–28: Rep rows 2–5 consecutively, ending with row 4.

Row 29: Ch 1, sk first vertical bar, sl st in each vertical bar across. Fasten off both colors.

Edging
Rnd 1: Working around entire outer edge with RS facing, with size I hook and Aran, join with sl st in first st of last row, sl st in each st across, ch 1, *evenly sp 13 sl sts across ends of rows, ch 1*, working in starting ch on opposite side of row 1, sl st in each ch across, ch 1, rep between *, join with sl st in beg sl st. *(13 sts across each side between corner chs)*

Rnd 2: Working this rnd in **back lps** only *(see Stitch Guide)*, ch 1, sc in each of first 3 sts, *[**sc dec** *(see Stitch Guide)* in next 2 sts, sc in each of next 3 sts] twice, ch 1, dc in next corner ch, ch 1**, sc in next 3 sts, rep from * around, ending last rep at **, join with sl st in beg sc, **turn**. Fasten off. *(11 sc and 2 chs across each side between corner dc)*

Rnd 3: Join light sage with sc in first ch sp after any corner dc, *ch 1, sk next st, [sc in next st, ch 1, sk next st] 5 times, sc in next ch sp, ch 3, sk next corner dc**, sc in next ch sp, rep from * around, ending last rep at **, join with sl st in beg sc, turn. Fasten off.

Rnd 4: Join Aran with sc in first st after any corner ch sp, *[working behind next ch sp, dc in next skipped st on rnd before last, sc in next st on last rnd] 6 times, working behind next corner ch sp, (dc, ch 3, dc) in next skipped corner dc on rnd before last**, sc in next st on last rnd, rep from * around, ending last rep at **, join with sl st in beg sc. Fasten off. *(15 sts across each side between corner ch sps)*

Block B
Make 30.
Using light sage instead of rose pink, work same as Block A. Predominantly light sage side of Block will be RS of work.

Edging
Using rose pink instead of light sage on rnd 3, work same as Block A's Edging.

Block C
Make 35.
Rnd 1: With I hook and rose pink, ch 4, 2 dc in 4th ch from hook, ch 3, ({3 dc, ch 3} 3 times) in same ch, join with sl st in 3rd ch of beg ch-3. Fasten off. *(12 dc, 4 ch sps)*

Rnd 2: Join light sage with sl st in any ch sp, ch 3 *(counts as first dc)*, (2 dc, ch 3, 3 dc) in same ch sp, ch 1, *(3 dc, ch 3, 3 dc) in next ch sp, ch 1,

rep from * around, join with sl st in 3rd ch of beg ch-3. Fasten off.

Rnd 3: Join rose pink with sl st in any ch-3 sp, ch 3, (2 dc, ch 3, 3 dc) in same ch sp, ch 1, 3 dc in next ch sp, ch 1, *(3 dc, ch 3, 3 dc) in next ch sp, ch 1, 3 dc in next ch sp, ch 1, rep from * around, join with sl st in 3rd ch of beg ch-3. Fasten off. *(8 ch-1 sps, 4 ch-3 sps)*

Rnd 4: Join Aran with sl st in any ch-3 sp, ch 3, (2 dc, ch 3, 3 dc) in same ch sp, ch 1, [3 dc in next ch sp, ch 1] twice, *(3 dc, ch 3, 3 dc) in next ch sp, ch 1, [3 dc in next ch sp, ch 1] twice, rep from * around, join with sl st in 3rd ch of beg ch-3. Fasten off. *(12 dc and 3 ch-1 sps across each side between corner ch-3 sps)*

Block D
Make 24.
Reversing rose pink and light sage, work same as Block C.

Holding Blocks WS tog, matching sts, with Aran, sew tog through back lps

C	A	C	A	C	A	C	A	C
B	D	B	D	B	D	B	D	B
C	A	C	A	C	A	C	A	C
B	D	B	D	B	D	B	D	B
C	A	C	A	C	A	C	A	C
B	D	B	D	B	D	B	D	B
C	A	C	A	C	A	C	A	C
B	D	B	D	B	D	B	D	B
C	A	C	A	C	A	C	A	C
B	D	B	D	B	D	B	D	B
C	A	C	A	C	A	C	A	C
B	D	B	D	B	D	B	D	B
C	A	C	A	C	A	C	A	C

Easter Afghan Assembly Illustration

in 9 rows of 13 Blocks each according to illustration.

BORDER
Rnd 1: Working around entire outer edge, join Aran with sc in any corner ch sp, ch 3, sc in same ch sp, *ch 1, sc in center st of next 3-dc group, ch 1, [sc in next ch sp, ch 1, sc in center st of next 3-dc group, ch 1] 3 times, **sc in next ch sp, ch 1, sk next seam, sc in next ch sp, ch 1, sk next st, [sc in next st, ch 1, sk next st] 7 times, sc in next ch sp, ch 1, sk next seam, sc in next ch sp, ch 1, sc in center st of next 3-dc group, ch 1, [sc in next ch sp, ch 1, sc in next center st of next 3-dc group, ch 1] 3 times, rep from ** across***, to next corner ch sp, (sc, ch 3, sc) in next ch sp, rep from * around, ending last rep at ***, join with sl st in beg sc. *(80 ch-1 sps across each short edge between corner ch-3 sps, 116 ch-1 sps across each long edge between corner ch-3 sps)*

Rnd 2: Sl st in first corner ch sp, ch 1, (sc, ch 3, sc) in same ch sp, ch 1, [sc in next ch sp, ch 1] across to next corner ch sp, *(sc, ch 3, sc) in next ch sp, ch 1, [sc in next ch sp, ch 1] across to next corner ch sp, rep from * around, join with sl st in beg sc.

Rnd 3: Sl st in first corner ch sp, ch 3, (2 dc, ch 3, 3 dc) in same ch sp, *ch 1, sk next ch sp, [3 dc in next ch sp, ch 1, sk next ch sp] across to next corner ch sp**, (3 dc, ch 3, 3 dc) in next ch sp, rep from * around, ending last rep at **, join with sl st in 3rd ch of beg ch-3.

Rnd 4: Ch 2, **dc dec** *(see Stitch Guide)* in next 2 sts, *horizontal cl* (see Special Stitches), (dc, horizontal cl, dc) in next corner ch sp, horizontal cl, [dc dec in next 3 sts, horizontal cl] across** to next corner ch sp, rep from * around, ending last rep at **, join with sl st in top of beg dc dec. Fasten off. ❏❏

Popcorn Paradise Afghan

Design by Christine Grazioso Moody

SKILL LEVEL

INTERMEDIATE

FINISHED SIZE
40 x 64½ inches

MATERIALS

- ❑ Medium (worsted) weight yarn:
    18 oz/900 yds/510g of various scrap colors of light and dark
    11 oz/550 yds/312g black
- ❑ Size I/9/5.5mm crochet hook
- ❑ Size J/10/6mm double-ended crochet hook or size needed to obtain gauge
- ❑ Tapestry needle

GAUGE
Double-ended hook: 7 sts = 2 inches; 4 pattern rows = 1 inch
Each Panel is 4 inches wide x 63 inches long, not including Edging

PATTERN NOTES
Read General Instructions on pages 3–5 before beginning pattern.

Use double-ended hook unless otherwise stated.

SPECIAL STITCH
Treble loop (tr lp): Yo twice, insert hook in bar specified in instructions, yo, pull through, [yo, pull through 2 lps on hook] twice.

INSTRUCTIONS

AFGHAN

Panel
Make 3.

Row 1: With dark scrap color, ch 15, pull up lp in 2nd ch from hook, pull up lp in next ch, ***tr lp** (see Special Stitch) in next ch, pull up lp in each of next 3 chs; rep from * across, turn. (15 lps on hook)

Row 2: With light scrap color, work lps off hook, **do not turn.**

Row 3: Ch 1, pull up lp in top strand of next 2 horizontal bars (see illustration), [tr in top strand of next horizontal

bar, pull up lp in top strand of next 3 horizontal bars] across, turn.

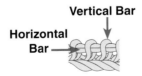

Row 4: With same dark color, work lps off hook, do not turn.

Row 5: Ch 1, pull up lp in top strand of next 2 horizontal bars, [tr in top strand of next horizontal bar, pull up lp in top strand of next 3 horizontal bars] across, turn.

Row 6: With same light color, work lps off hook, do not turn.

Row 7: Ch 1, pull up lp in top strand

of next 2 horizontal bars, [tr lp in top strand of next horizontal bar, pull up lp in top strand of next 3 horizontal bars] across, turn.

Rows 8–27: Rep rows 4–7 consecutively.

Row 28: With next dark scrap color, work lps off hook, do not turn.

Row 29: Ch 1, pull up lp in top strand of next 2 horizontal bars, [tr lp in top strand of next horizontal bar, pull up lp in top strand of next 3 horizontal bars] across, turn.

Row 30: With next light scrap color, work lps off hook, do not turn.

Row 31: Ch 1, pull up lp in top strand of next 2 horizontal bars, [tr lp in top strand of next horizontal bar, pull up lp in top strand of next 3 horizontal bars] across, turn.

Row 32: With same dark scrap color, work lps off hook, do not turn.

Row 33: Ch 1, pull up lp in top strand of next 2 horizontal bars, [tr lp in top strand of next horizontal bar, pull up lp in top strand of next 3 horizontal bars] across, turn.

Row 34: With same light scrap color, work lps off hook, do not turn.

Row 35: Ch 1, pull up lp in top strand of next 2 horizontal bars, [tr lp in top strand of next horizontal bar, pull up lp in top strand of next 3 horizontal bars] across, turn.

Rows 36–55: Rep rows 32–35 consecutively.

Rows 56–251: Rep rows 28–55 consecutively.

Row 252: With same light scrap color, work lps off hook. Fasten off.

First Side Edging

Row 1: With light color side facing, working in end of rows across 1 long edge, with size I hook, join black with sl st in last row, ch 3, evenly sp 188 dc across, turn. *(189 dc)*

Row 2: Ch 4, sk next st, dc in next st, [ch 1, sk next st, dc in next st] across, turn.

Row 3: Ch 3, dc in each ch sp and in each st across. Fasten off.

2nd Side Edging

Working on opposite long edge of same Panel, starting in row 1, work same as First Side Edging.

Assembly

Matching sts on long edges, sew Panels tog.

End Edging

With RS facing, with size I hook and black, starting at top right corner, join with sl st in end of row 3 on Side Edging, ch 3, evenly sp 131 dc across. Fasten off.

Rep End Edging on opposite end. ❑❑

Killarny Scalloped Stole

Design by Joyce Nordstrom

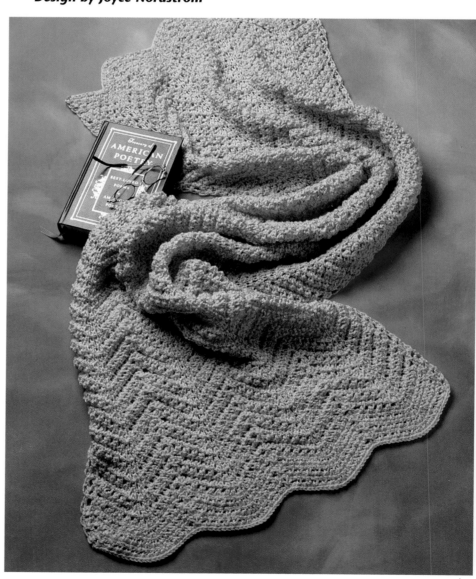

SKILL LEVEL

INTERMEDIATE

FINISHED SIZE

24 x 70 inches

MATERIALS

❑ Medium (worsted) weight yarn:
   11 oz/550 yds/312g each of Aran and flecked
❑ Size J/10/6mm double-ended crochet hook or size needed to obtain gauge

GAUGE

7 sts = 2 inches

PATTERN NOTE

Read General Instructions on pages 3–5 before beginning pattern.

SPECIAL STITCHES

Open single crochet loop (open sc lp): Yo, sk next vertical bar, pull up lp in next vertical bar, yo, pull through 1 lp on hook.

4 stitch decrease (4 st dec): [Sk next vertical bar, pull up lp in next vertical bar] twice, yo, pull through 2 lps on hook, yo, pull through 1 lp on hook.

Double decrease (dbl dec): Yo, [sk next vertical bar, pull up lp in next vertical bar] 3 times, yo, pull through 3 lps on hook, yo, pull through 1 lp on hook.

INSTRUCTIONS
STOLE
Row 1: With Aran, ch 109, pull up lp in 2nd ch from hook, pull up lp in each ch across, turn. *(109 lps on hook)*

Row 2: With flecked, work lps off hook, **do not turn.**

Row 3: Ch 1, sk first **vertical bar** *(see illustration)*, yo, [sk next vertical bar, pull up lp in next vertical bar] twice, yo, pull through 2 lps on hook, yo, pull through 1 lp on hook *(dec made)*, *[yo, sk next vertical bar, pull up lp in next vertical bar] 4 times, [yo, pull up lp in next vertical bar] 4 times, [yo, sk next vertical bar, pull up lp next vertical bar] 4 times**, yo, [sk next vertical bar, pull up lp in next vertical bar] 3 times, yo, pull through 3 lps on hook, yo, pull through 1 lp on hook *(dec made)*, rep from * across, ending last rep at **, yo, [sk next vertical bar, pull up lp in next vertical bar] twice, yo, pull through 2

Vertical Bar

Horizontal Bar

lps on hook, yo, pull through 1 lp on hook, yo, sk next vertical bar, pull up lp in last verticalbar, turn.

Row 4: With Aran, work lps off hook, do not turn.

Row 5: Ch 1, sk first vertical bar, pull up lp in each vertical bar and in each lp across, turn. *(109 lps on hook)*

Rows 6–14: Rep rows 2–5 consecutively, ending with row 2.

Row 15: Ch 1, sk first vertical bar, yo, **4 st dec** *(see Special Stitches)*, ***open sc lp** *(see Special Stitches)* 4 times, [yo, pull up lp in next vertical bar] 4 times, open sc lp 4 times**, **dbl dec** *(see Special Stitches)*, rep from * across, ending last rep at **, yo, 4 st dec, yo, sk next vertical bar, pull up lp in last vertical bar, turn.

Row 16: With Aran, work lps off hook, do not turn.

Row 17: Ch 1, sk first vertical bar, yo, 4 st dec, *open sc lp 4 times, [yo, pull up lp in next vertical bar] 4 times, open sc lp 4 times**, dbl dec, rep from * across, ending last rep at **, yo, 4 st dec, yo, sk next vertical bar, pull up lp in last vertical bar, turn.

Row 18: With flecked yarn, work lps off hook, do not turn.

Rows 19–196: Rep rows 15–18 consecutively, ending with row 16 and Aran.

Row 197: Ch 1, sk first vertical bar, pull up lp in each vertical bar across, turn *(109 lps on hook)*

Row 198: With flecked yarn, work lps off hook, do not turn.

Row 199: Ch 1, sk first vertical bar, yo, [sk next vertical bar, pull up lp in next vertical bar] twice, yo, pull through 2 lps on hook, yo, pull through 1 lp on hook *(dec made)*, *[yo, sk next vertical bar, pull up lp in next vertical bar] 4 times, [yo, pull up lp in next vertical bar] 4 times, [yo, sk next vertical bar, pull up lp next vertical bar] 4 times**, yo, [sk next vertical bar, pull up lp in next vertical bar] 3 times, yo, pull through 3 lps on hook, yo, pull through 1 lp on hook *(dec made)*, rep from * across, ending last rep at **, yo, [sk next vertical bar, pull up lp in next vertical bar] twice, yo, pull through 2 lps on hook, yo, pull through 1 lp on hook, yo, sk next vertical bar, pull up lp in last vertical bar, turn.

Row 200: With Aran, work lps off hook, do not turn.

Row 201: Ch 1, sk first vertical bar, pull up lp in each vertical bar across, turn.

Rows 202–208: Rep rows 198–201 consecutively, ending with row 200.

Row 209: Ch 1, sl st in each vertical bar across. Fasten off. ❏❏

Monoghan Poncho

Design by Joyce Nordstrom

SKILL LEVEL

EXPERIENCED

FINISHED SIZES

Instructions given fit size small/ medium, with changes for large/ X-large in [ ].

MATERIALS

- ❏ Medium (worsted) weight yarn: 12 [14] oz/600 [700] yds/ 340 [397]g each gray and white
- ❏ Size K/10½/6.5mm double-ended crochet hook or size needed to obtain gauge
- ❏ Size I/9/5.5mm crochet hook or size needed to obtain gauge
- ❏ Tapestry needle
- ❏ Stitch markers

4 MEDIUM

GAUGE

Double-ended hook: 7 sts = 2 inches, 12 pattern rows = 2¾ inches

PATTERN NOTE

Read General Instructions on pages 3–5 before beginning pattern.

SPECIAL STITCHES

Single crochet loop (sc lp): Pull up lp in specified bar or st, yo, pull through 1 lp on hook.

Treble crochet loop (tr lp): Yo twice, insert hook in specified st or bar, yo, pull lp through, [yo, pull through 2 lps on hook] twice. Sk next vertical bar on last row behind tr lp.

Gray cable: Sk first post st of next 2 post st group, **fpdtr** *(see Stitch Guide)* around next post st, pull up lp in each of next 2 vertical bars on last row, fpdtr around sk post st.

White cable: Sk first post st of next 2 post st group, fpdtr around next post st, sc lp in each of next 2 vertical bars on last row, fpdtr around sk post st.

INSTRUCTIONS

PONCHO

Panel

Make 2.

Row 1: With double-ended hook and gray, ch 78, pull up lp in 2nd ch from hook, pull up lp in each ch across, turn. *(78 lps on hook)*

Row 2: With white, work lps off hook, **do not turn.**

Row 3: Ch 1, sk first vertical bar, **sc lp** *(see Special Stitches)* in each vertical bar across, turn.

Row 4: With gray, work lps off hook, do not turn.

Row 5: Ch 1, sk first vertical bar, pull up lp in each of next 9 vertical bars, ***tr lp** *(see Special Stitches)* in corresponding st on row 2, pull up lp in each of next 2

vertical bars on last row, sk next 2 sts on row 2, tr lp in next st, pull up lp in each of next 4 vertical bars on last row, tr lp in corresponding st on row 2, pull up lp in each of next 2 vertical bars on last row, sk next 2 sts on row 2, tr lp in next st*, pull up lp in each of next 34 vertical bars on last row, rep between *, pull up lp in each of last 10 vertical bars on last row, turn.

Row 6: With white, work lps off hook, do not turn.

Row 7: Ch 1, sk first vertical bar, sc lp in each of next 9 vertical bars, *tr lp in vertical bar of corresponding st 4 rows below, sc lp in each of next 2 vertical bars on last row, sk next 2 sts 4 rows below, tr lp in vertical bar of next st, sc lp in each of next 4 vertical bars on last row, tr lp in vertical bar of corresponding st 4 rows below, sc lp in each of next 2 vertical bars of last row, sk next 2 sts 4 rows below, tr lp in next st*, sc lp in each of next 34 vertical bars on last row, rep between *, sc lp in each of last 10 vertical bars on last row, turn.

Row 8: With gray, work lps off hook, do not turn.

Row 9: Ch 1, sk first vertical bar, pull up lp in each of next 9 vertical bars, *work **gray cable** (see Special Stitches), pull up lp in each of next 4 vertical bars, work gray cable*, pull up lp in each of next 34 vertical bars, rep between *, pull up lp in each of last 10 vertical bars, turn.

Row 10: With white, work lps off hook, do not turn.

Row 11: Ch 1, sk first vertical bar, sc lp in each of next 9 vertical bars, *work **white cable** (see Special Stitches), sc lp in each of next 4 vertical bars, work white cable*, sc lp in each of next 34 vertical bars, rep between *, sc lp in each of last 10 vertical bars, turn.

Row 12: With gray, work lps off hook, do not turn.

Row 13: Ch 1, sk first vertical bar, pull up lp in each of next 9 vertical bars, *tr lp around post of first st of next 2-post st group, pull up lp in each of next 2 vertical bars on last row, tr lp around post of next st of same group, pull up lp in each of next 4 vertical bars on last row, tr lp around post of first st of next 2-post st group, pull up lp in each of next 2 vertical bars on last row, tr lp around post of next st of same group*, pull up lp in each of next 34 vertical bars on last row, rep between *, pull up lp in each of last 10 vertical bars, turn.

Row 14: With white, work lps off hook, do not turn.

Row 15: Ch 1, sk first vertical bar, sc lp in each of next 9 vertical bars, *tr lp around post of first st of next 2-post st group, sc lp in each of next 2 vertical bars on last row, tr lp around post of next st of same group, sc lp in each of next 4 vertical bars on last row, tr lp around post of first st of next 2-post st group, sc lp in each of next 2 vertical bars on last row, tr lp around post of next st of same group*, sc lp in each of next 34 vertical bars on last row, rep between *, sc lp in each of last 10 vertical bars on last row, turn.

Rows 16–122 [16–130]: Rep rows 8–15 consecutively, ending with row 10.

Row 123 [131]: Sl st in first 10 vertical bars, ***fpdtr** (see Stitch Guide) around post of 2nd st of next 2-post st group, sl st in each of next 2 vertical bars on last row, fpdtr around post of first st of same group, sl st in each of next 4 vertical bars on last row, fpdtr around post of 2nd st of next 2-post st group, sl st in each of next 2 vertical bars on last row, fpdtr around post of first st of same group*, sl st in each of next 34 vertical bars on last row, rep between *, sl st in each of last 10 vertical bars on last row. Fasten off.

ASSEMBLY

With predominantly gray side of Panels facing, place stitch marker 7 [8½] inches below upper right corner on each Panel. Place end of 2nd Panel against side of First Panel, (see letter A on assembly illustration). Working through both thicknesses and easing to fit, with size I hook and gray, join with sc in first st to the left, working from left to right, [ch 1, sk next st, **reverse sc** in next st (see illustration) across. Fasten off.

Place end of first Panel against side of 2nd Panel (see letter B on assembly illustration), join in same manner stopping at marker. Do not fasten off. Working in sts and in ends of rows around neck opening, evenly sp sts so piece lies flat, [ch 1, sk next st or row, reverse sc in next st or row] around, sl st in seam. Fasten off. ❏❏

Assembly Illustration

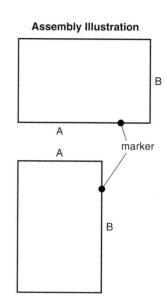

Reverse Single Crochet

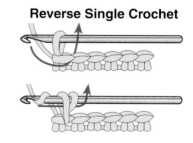

Jacket Elegance

Design by Ann Parnell

SKILL LEVEL
EXPERIENCED

FINISHED SIZES
Instructions given fit 36-inch bust (*small*), changes for 39-inch bust (*medium*), 41-inch bust (*large*) and 46-inch bust (*X-large*) busts are in [ ].

MATERIALS

- ❑ Bulky (chunky) weight yarn:
   12 [13, 14, 16] oz/360 [390, 420, 480] yds/340 [369, 397, 454]g each rose and variegated
- ❑ Size H/8/5mm double-ended swivel crochet hook or size needed to obtain gauge
- ❑ Size H/8/5mm crochet hook
- ❑ Tapestry needle

GAUGE
Double-ended hook: 5 pattern sts = 2½ inches, 6 pattern rows = 1 inch

PATTERN NOTES
Read General Instructions on pages 3–5 before beginning pattern.

Use double-ended hook unless otherwise stated.

Jacket is worked in 1 piece from Sleeve to Sleeve.

INSTRUCTIONS
JACKET
Row 1: Starting at bottom of 1 Sleeve, with variegated, ch 35, pull up lp in 2nd ch from hook and in each ch across leaving all lps on hook, turn. *(35 lps on hook)*

Row 2: With rose, yo, pull through 1 lp on hook, [ch 1, yo, pull through 3 lps on hook] across, **do not turn.**

Row 3: Ch 1, sk first 2 vertical bars, pull up lp in next ch sp, [yo, pull up lp in next ch sp] across to last vertical bar, pull up lp in last vertical bar, turn.

Rows 4 & 5: With variegated, rep rows 2 and 3.

Row 6: Rep row 2.

Row 7: For **inc**, ch 2, pull up lp in 2nd ch from hook, [yo, pull up lp in next ch sp] across to last vertical bar, pull up lp in last vertical bar, turn. *(37 lps on hook)*

Row 8: With variegated, rep row 2.

Row 9: Rep row 7. *(39 lps on hook)*

Small and Medium Sizes Only

Rows 10–13 [10–13]: Rep rows 2–5.

Rows 14–73 [14–73]: Rep rows 2–13 consecutively, ending with 59 lps on hook in last row.

Large and X–large Sizes Only

Rows [10–73, 10–73]: Rep rows 2–9 consecutively, ending with 71 lps on hook in last row.

For All Sizes

Rows 74–102: Rep rows 2–5 consecutively, ending with row 2. At end of last row, ch 50, pull up long lp to be picked up later. Join a separate strand of rose in other end of last row, ch 50. Fasten off.

Body

Row 103: Pick up dropped lp, pull up lp in 2nd ch from hook, pull up lp in each of next 48 chs, pull up lp in each of first 2 vertical bars of Sleeve, [yo, pull up lp in next ch sp] across to last vertical bar, pull up lp in last vertical bar, pull up lp in each of next 50 chs, turn. *(159 [159, 171, 171] lps on hook)*

Rows 104 & 105: Rep rows 4 and 5.

Rows 106–142 [106–146, 106–150, 106–158]: Rep rows 2–5 consecutively, ending with row 2.

Back Neck Shaping

Row 143 [147, 151, 159]: Ch 1, sk first 2 vertical bars, pull up lp in next ch sp, [yo, pull up lp in next ch sp] 38 [38, 41, 41] times, pull up lp in next 2 vertical bars at same time leaving rem sts unworked forming first front section, turn. *(79 [79, 85, 85] lps on hook)*

Rows 144 & 145 [148 & 149, 152 & 153, 160 & 161]: Rep rows 4 and 5.

Rows 146–182 [150–186, 154–190, 162–198]: Rep rows 2–5 consecutively, ending with row 2. At end of

last row, pull up long lp to be picked up later. Join a separate strand of rose in last st at other end of row, ch 80 [80, 86, 86] forming 2nd front section, fasten off.

Row 183 [187, 191, 199]: Pick up dropped lp at beg of row, ch 1, sk first 2 vertical bars, pull up lp in next ch sp, [yo, pull up lp in next ch sp] across to last vertical bar, pull up lp in last vertical bar, pull up lp in each of next 80 [80, 86, 86] chs, turn. *(159 [159, 171, 171] lps on hook)*

Rows 184 & 185 [188 & 189, 192 & 193, 200 & 201]: Rep rows 4 and 5.

Rows 186–222 [190–230, 194–238, 202–254]: Rep rows 2–5 consecutively, ending with row 2. At end of last row, fasten off.

2nd Sleeve

Row 223 [231, 239, 255]: Join rose with sl st in 25th ch sp, [yo, pull up lp in next ch sp] 29 [29, 35, 35] times leaving rem ch sps unworked, turn. *(59 [59, 71, 71] lps on hook)*

Rows 224 & 225 [232 & 233, 240 & 241, 256 & 257]: Rep rows 4 and 5.

Rows 226–254 [234–262, 242–270, 258–-286]: Rep rows 2–5 consecutively, ending with row 2.

Row 255 [263, 271, 287]: Ch 1, sk first 2 vertical bars, for **dec**, [pull up lp in next ch sp] 3 times, [yo, pull up lp in next ch sp] across to last vertical bar, pull up lp in last vertical bar, turn. *(57 [57, 69, 69] lps on hook)*

Row 256 [264, 272, 288]: Rep row 4.

Row 257 [265, 273, 289]: Rep row 255 [263, 271, 287]. *(55 [55, 67, 67] lps on hook)*

Rows 258–265 [266–273, 274–277, 290–293]: Rep rows 2–5 consecutively.

Row 266 [274, 278, 294]: Rep row 2.

Rows 267–269 [275–277, 279–281, 295–297]: Rep row 255 [263, 271, 287] and row 4 alternately, ending with row 255 [263, 271, 287] and 51 [51, 63, 63] lps on hook in last row.

Rows 270–277 [278–285, 282–285, 298–301]: Rep rows 2–5 consecutively.

Rows 278–323 [286–331, 286–339, 302–355]: Rep rows 266–277 [274–285, 278–285, 294–301] consecutively, ending with row 275 [283, 283, 299]

and 35 lps on hook in last row.

Row 324 [332, 340, 356]: With variegated, ch 1, sk first 2 vertical bars, sl st in next ch sp, [ch 1, sl st in next ch sp] across to last vertical bar, sl st in last vertical bar. Fasten off.

Sew Sleeve/side seams, leaving 5 inches unsewn on bottom of each side for slit.

FRONT BAND

Row 1: Working across front and neck of Jacket, join variegated with sl st in first st at bottom of Jacket, ch 1, pull up lp in each st across first front, working in ends of rows, pull up lp in each "stripe" across neck, pull up lp in each st across 2nd front, turn.

Row 2: With rose, pull through 1 lp on hook, [yo, pull through 2 lps on hook across, do not turn.

Row 3: Ch 1, sk first vertical bar, pull up lp in top strand of each **horizontal bar** *(see illustration)* across, turn.

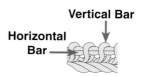

Vertical Bar

Horizontal Bar →

Row 4: With variegated, rep row 2.

Row 5: Ch 1, sk first vertical bar, pull up lp in top strand of each horizontal bar across, turn.

Rows 6–26: Rep rows 2–5 consecutively, ending with row 2. At end of last row, fasten off.

EDGING

Bottom Edging

With predominantly variegated side facing, working in ends of rows and in sts across bottom of Jacket, evenly sp sts so piece lies flat, with size H hook and variegated, join with sc in last row on Front Band, sc across bottom of Jacket including slit edges across to opposite corner with 3 sc in each corner of slits. Fasten off.

Sleeve Edging

With predominantly variegated side facing, working around bottom edge of Sleeve, with size H hook and variegated, join with sc in Sleeve seam, sc evenly sp around Sleeve, join with sl st in beg sc. Fasten off.

Rep around rem Sleeve. ❏❏

Cross-Stitch Vest

Design by Margret Willson

FINISHED SIZES

Instructions given fit 34-inch bust (*small*), changes for 39-inch bust (*medium*) and 44-inch bust (*large*) are in [ ].

MATERIALS

❑ Medium (worsted) yarn:
   12 [13, 14] oz/600 [650, 700] yds/340 [369, 397]g rose
   8 [9, 10] oz/400 [450, 500] yds/ 227 [255, 284]g Aran
❑ Size G/6/4mm double-ended swivel crochet hook or size needed to obtain gauge
❑ Size G/6/4mm crochet hook or size needed to obtain gauge
❑ Tapestry needle

GAUGES

Double-ended hook: 4 dc lps = 1 inch; 8 pattern rows = 2 inches
Size G hook: 4 sts = 1 inch

PATTERN NOTES

Read General Instructions on pages 3–5 before beginning pattern.
Use double-ended hook unless otherwise stated.
Vest is worked in 1 piece to underarms.

SPECIAL STITCHES

Double crochet knit (dc k): Yo, insert hook between front and back vertical bars and under horizontal bar of next st (*see illustration*) yo, pull lp through, yo, pull through 2 lps on hook.

Double Crochet Knit Stitch

Cross-stitch (cross-st): Sk next vertical bar, pull up lp in next vertical bar, pull up lp in last skipped vertical bar.

Ending decrease (end dec): Yo, pull through 2 lps on hook.

Beginning decrease (beg dec): Dc k in next vertical bar, yo, pull through 2 lps on hook.

INSTRUCTIONS

VEST

Row 1: With aran, ch 146 [164, 184], pull up lp in 2nd ch from hook and in each ch across, turn. *(146 [164, 184] lps on hook)*

Row 2: With rose, work lps off hook, **do not turn.**

Row 3: Ch 1, sk first vertical bar, **dc K** *(see Special Stitches)* across, turn.

Row 4: With Aran, work lps off hook, do not turn.

Row 5: Ch 1, sk first vertical bar, **cross-st** *(see Special Stitches)* across to last vertical bar, pull up lp in last vertical bar, turn.

Row 6: With rose, work lps off hook, do not turn.

Row 7: Ch 1, sk first vertical bar, dc K across, turn.

Row 8: With Aran, work lps off hook, do not turn.

Row 9: Ch 1, sk first vertical bar, dc K across, turn.

Rows 10–50 [10–58, 10–58]: Rep rows 2–9 consecutively, ending with row 2.

First Front

Row 51 [59, 59]: Ch 1, sk first vertical bar, dc k 29 [33, 37] times leaving rem sts unworked, turn. *(30 [34, 38] lps on hook)*

Row 52 [60, 60]: With Aran, work lps off hook, do not turn.

Row 53 [61, 61]: Rep row 5.

Row 54 [62, 62]: With rose, work lps off hook, do not turn.

Neck Shaping

Row 55 [63, 63]: Ch 1, sk first vertical bar, **beg dec** *(see Special Stitches)*, dc k across, turn. Decreases form Neck Shaping on front. *(29 [33, 37] lps on hook)*

Row 56 [64, 64]: With Aran, work lps off hook, do not turn.

Row 57 [65, 65]: Ch 1, sk first vertical bar, dc k across, **end dec** *(see Special Stitches)*, turn. *(28 [32, 36] lps on hook)*

Row 58 [66, 66]: With rose, work lps off hook, do not turn.

Row 59 [67, 67]: Ch 1, sk first vertical bar, beg dec, dc k across, turn. *(27 [31, 35] lps on hook)*

Row 60 [68, 68]: With Aran, work lps off hook, do not turn.

Row 61 [69, 69]: Ch 1, sk first vertical bar, cross-st across, turn.

Row 62 [70, 70]: With rose, work lps off hook, do not turn.

Row 63 [71, 71]: Rep row 59 [67, 67]. *(26 [30, 34] lps on hook)*

Row 64 [72, 72]: With Aran, work lps off hook, do not turn.

Row 65 [73, 73]: Ch 1, sk first vertical bar, dc k across, end dec, turn. *(25 [29, 33] lps on hook)*

Row 66 [74, 74]: With rose, work lps off hook, do not turn.

Row 67 [75, 75]: Rep row 59 [67, 67]. *(24 [28, 32] lps on hook)*

Row 68 [76, 76]: With Aran, work lps off hook, do not turn.

Row 69 [77, 77]: Ch 1, sk first vertical bar, cross-st across to last vertical bar, pull up lp in last vertical bar, turn.

Row 70 [78, 78]: With rose, work lps off hook, do not turn.

Row 71 [79, 79]: Rep row 59 [67, 67]. *(23 [27, 31] lps on hook)*

Row 72 [80, 80]: With Aran, work lps off hook, do not turn.

Row 73 [81, 81]: Rep row 65 [73, 73]. *(22 [26, 30] lps on hook)*

Rows 74–95 [82–103, 82–97]: Rep rows 58–73 [66–81, 66–81] consecutively, ending with row 63 [71, 81] and 14 [18, 24] lps on hook in last row.

Large Size Only

Rows [98–103]: Rep rows 2–7.

All Sizes Only

Row 96 [104, 104]: Ch 1, sl st in each vertical bar across. Fasten off.

Back

Row 51 [59, 59]: With rose, for **armhole,** sl st in each of next 15 [15, 17] unworked vertical bars of row 50 [58, 58], ch 1, dc k in each of next 57 [67, 75] vertical bars leaving rem sts unworked, turn. *(58 [68, 76] lps on hook)*

Rows 52–57 [60–65, 60–65]: Rep rows 4–9.

Rows 58–95 [66–103, 66–103]: Rep rows 2–9 consecutively, ending with row 7.

Row 96 [104, 104]: Ch 1, sl st in each vertical bar across. Fasten off.

2nd Front

Row 51 [59, 59]: For **armhole,** with rose, sl st in each of next 15 [15, 17] unworked vertical bars of row 50 [58, 58], ch 1, dc k in each of last 29 [33, 37] vertical bars, turn. *(30 [34, 38] lps on hook)*

Rows 52–96 [60–104, 60–104]: Rep same rows of First Front, reversing beg and end dec.

Sew shoulder seams.

Armhole

Rnd 1: Working in ends of rows and in sts around 1 Armhole, with size G hook, join rose with sc in center of underarm, evenly sp sc so piece lies flat, sc around, join with sl st in beg sc.

Rnd 2: Ch 3 *(counts as first dc)*, dc in each st around with **dc dec** *(see Stitch Guide)* in next 3 sts at each corner of underarm, join with sl st in 3rd ch of beg ch-3.

Rnd 3: Ch 1, sc in each st around with **sc dec** *(see Stitch Guide)* in next 2 sts at each corner of underarm, join with sl st in beg sc. Fasten off.

Rep around rem Armhole.

Edging

Rnd 1: Working in ends of rows and in sts around entire Vest, with size G hook, join rose with sc in center back of neck, evenly sp sc so piece lies flat, sc around with 3 sc in each bottom corner, join with sl st in beg sc.

Rnd 2: Ch 3, dc in each st around with dc dec in next 3 sts at each shoulder seam, 2 dc at base of each Neck Shaping *(row 49 [57, 57])* and 5 dc in center st of each bottom corner, join with sl st in 3rd ch of beg ch-3.

Rnd 3: Ch 1, sc in each st around with [sc dec in next 2 sts] at each shoulder seam, 2 sc at base of each Neck Shaping and 3 sc in center st of each bottom corner, join with sl st in beg sc. Fasten off. ❑❑

Crochet on the Double Poncho

Design by Agnes Russell

SKILL LEVEL

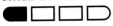

BEGINNER

FINISHED SIZE
Girl's 8–10

MATERIALS
- ❏ Bulky (chunky) weight yarn:(3½ oz/106 yds/99g per ball):
    2 balls each solid color *(MC)* and variegated color *(CC)*
- ❏ Size P/15mm double-ended crochet hook or size needed to obtain gauge
- ❏ Size P/15mm crochet hook
- ❏ Tapestry needle
- ❏ 5-inch square of cardboard

GAUGE
4 sts = 2 inches

PATTERN NOTES
Read General Instructions on pages 3–5 before beginning pattern.

Poncho is crocheted in 2 simple strips.

INSTRUCTIONS
PONCHO
FIRST HALF
Row 1: With P hook and MC, ch 25, pull up lp in 2nd ch from hook, pull up lp in each ch across turn. *(125 lps on hook)*

Row 2: With CC, work lps off hook, **do not turn.**

Row 3: Sk first vertical bar, pull up lp in each vertical bar across, turn.

Row 4: With MC, work lps off hook, do not turn.

Row 5: Sk first vertical bar, pull up lp in each vertical bar across turn.

Row 6: With CC, work lps off hook, do not turn.

Row 7: Sk first vertical bar, pull up lp in each vertical bar across turn.

Rows 8–102: Rep rows 4–7.

Row 103: With CC, sk first vertical bar, sl st in each vertical bar across. Fasten off.

2nd Half
Row 1: With predominantly MC facing and using diagram as a guide, beg with row 1 of First Half, make slip knot with MC and pick up 25 lps along edge as indicated.

Rows 2–103: Rep rows 2–103 of First Half.

With predominantly MC facing and using diagram as guide, sew seam joining at A and B.

BOTTOM TRIM
Rnd 1: With predominantly CC facing, join MC at back seam, with size P hook, ch 1, sc evenly sp around, working 3 sc in each corner, join with sl st in beg sc. Fasten off.

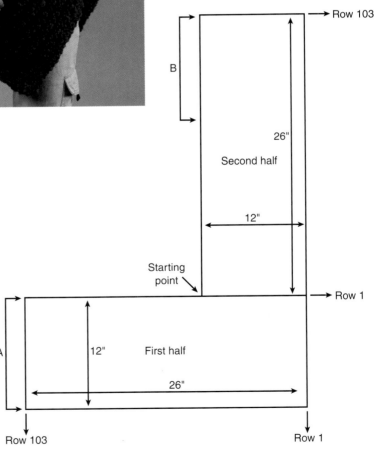

Poncho Diagram

NECKLINE TRIM

Rnd 1: This edging is designed to create a rolled edging around neckline, with predominantly CC side facing, with size P hook, join MC with sl st in any row at neckline opening, ch 1, work 52 sc evenly sp around neckline opening, join with sl st in beg sc. *(52 sc)*

Rnds 2–4: Working in **front lps** *(see Stitch Guide)* only, sl st in each st around. At the end of last rnd, fasten off.

Rnd 5: Turn Poncho inside out. With size P hook, join MC with sl st in rem free lp of rnd 1 of neckline trim, working with a slightly tighter tension to give neck stability, sl st in each st around. Fasten off.

TIE

With CC and size P hook, leaving 6-inch length at beg, ch 50, leaving 6-inch length, fasten off. Fold Tie in half, insert hook at center front of Poncho in rnd 2 of Neckline Trim, pull fold through to form lp on hook, pull ends through lp on hook, pull to secure.

POMPOM
Make 2.

From cardboard, cut 2 circles 2¼ inches in diameter, cut 1-inch hole in center of each circle. Holding the cardboard circles tog, wrap CC yarn around the cardboard circles until center hole is filled. Insert scissors between layers of cardboard circles, gently cut around outer edge between circles. Cut separate length of CC yarn, place between cardboard circles, pull ends tightly and knot to secure. Remove cardboard circles and attach Pom-pom to end of Tie.

Make 2nd Pompom and attach to rem end of Tie. ❏❏

Denim Delight

Design by Jennifer McClain

SKILL LEVEL

INTERMEDIATE

FINISHED SIZE
21 x 67¼ inches, including Fringe

MATERIALS
❏ Fine (sport) weight yarn: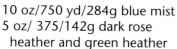
  10 oz/750 yd/284g blue mist
  5 oz/ 375/142g dark rose heather and green heather
❏ Size H/8/5mm double-ended swivel crochet hook or size needed to obtain gauge
❏ Size G/6/4mm crochet hook

GAUGE
Double-end hook, 4 sts = 1 inch; 6 pattern rows = 1 inch

PATTERN NOTE
Read General Instructions on pages 3–5 before beginning pattern.

SPECIAL STITCH
Single crochet loop (sc lp): Insert hook in next ch or vertical bar, yo, pull lp through, yo, pull through 1 lp on hook.

INSTRUCTIONS
SHAWL
Row 1: With double-ended hook and blue mist, ch 270, **sc lp** *(see Special Stitch)* in 2nd ch from hook, [pull up lp in next ch, sc lp in next ch] across, turn. *(270 lps on hook)*

Row 2: With rose, work lps off hook, **do not turn.**

Row 3: Sk first vertical bar, sc lp in next vertical bar, [pull up lp in next vertical bar, sc lp in next vertical bar] across, turn.

Rows 4–33: Working in color sequence of blue mist, green heather, blue mist, dark rose heather, blue mist, blue mist, blue mist, green heather, blue mist, dark rose heather, blue mist, green heather, blue mist, blue mist, blue mist, rep rows 2 and 3 alternately.

Rows 34–124: Rep rows 2–33 consecutively, ending with row 28.

Row 125: With size G hook, ch 1, sc in next vertical bar, [sl st in next vertical bar, sc in next vertical bar] across. Fasten off.

FRINGE
Cut 1 strand 11 inches in length the color of color section. Fold strand in half, insert hook in end of color section, pull fold through, pull all loose ends through fold. Tighten. Trim to 5 inches.

Attach Fringe in end of each color section on each short edge of Shawl. ❏❏

Twilight Slippers

Design by Debbie Tabor

SKILL LEVEL

INTERMEDIATE

FINISHED SIZE
12-inch sole

MATERIALS
- Bulky (chunky) weight yarn:
  2 oz/60 yds/57g variegated
- Medium (worsted) weight yarn:
  2 oz/100 yds/57g plum
- Size J/10/6mm double-ended crochet hook or size needed to obtain gauge
- Tapestry needle

GAUGE
4 sts = 1 inch; 6 pattern rows = 1 inch

PATTERN NOTE
Read General Instructions on pages 3–5 before beginning pattern.

INSTRUCTIONS
SLIPPER
Make 2.
Sole
Row 1: With plum, ch 27, pull up lp in 2nd ch from hook and in each ch across turn. *(27 lps on hook)*

Row 2: With variegated, work lps off hook, **do not turn.**

Row 3: Ch 1, sk first vertical bar, pull up lp in top strand of next 2 horizontal bars *(see illustration)*, [pull up lp in next 3 vertical bars at same time, pull up lp in top strand of next horizontal bar, pull up lp in next vertical bar, pull up lp in top strand of next horizontal bar] across, turn.

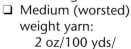

Vertical Bar

Horizontal Bar

Row 4: With plum, work lps off hook, do not turn.

Row 5: Rep row 3.

Rows 6–24: Rep rows 2–5 consecutively, ending with row 4.

Row 25: Ch 1, sk first vertical bar, pull up lp in top strand of each horizontal bar across, turn.

Row 26: With variegated, work lps off hook, do not turn.

Row 27: Ch 1, sk first vertical bar, pull up lp in top strand of each horizontal bar across, turn.

Row 28: With plum, work lps off hook, do not turn.

Rows 29–36: Rep rows 25–28 consecutively.

Row 37: Rep row 3.

Rows 38–64: Rep rows 2–5 consecutively, ending with row 4. At end of last row, leaving long plum end for sewing, fasten off both colors.

Toe
Thread plum yarn through sts of last row, pull tight to gather, secure.

Heel
Fold row 1 in half, matching sts, sew tog.

Vamp
Row 1: With plum, ch 23, pull up lp in 2nd ch from hook and in each ch across leaving all lps on hook, turn. *(23 lps on hook)*

Row 2: With variegated, work lps off hook, do not turn.

Row 3: Ch 1, sk first vertical bar, pull up lp in top strand of each horizontal bar across, turn.

Row 4: With plum, work lps off hook, do not turn.

Row 5: Ch 1, sk first vertical bar, pull up lp in top strand of each horizontal bar across, turn.

Rows 6–36: Rep rows 2–5 consecutively, ending with row 4. At end of last row, leaving long plum end for sewing, fasten off.

Vamp Toe
Weave plum through ends of rows on 1 end, pull tight to gather, secure.

Cuff
Row 1: With plum, ch 6, pull up lp in 2nd ch from hook and in each ch across, turn. *(6 lps on hook)*

Row 2: With variegated, work lps off hook, do not turn.

Row 3: Ch 1, sk first vertical bar, pull up lp under both strands of each horizontal bar across, turn.

Row 4: With plum, work lps off hook, do not turn.

Row 5: Ch 1, sk first vertical bar, pull up lp under both strands of each horizontal bar across, turn.

Rows 6–52: Rep rows 2–5 consecutively, ending with row 4. At end of last row, fasten off both colors.

Assembly
Matching Toes, sew sides of Sole and Vamp tog leaving 1 inch on each side of Vamp unsewn. Easing to fit, sew ends and 1 long edge of Cuff to the 1 inch of Vamp left unsewn and to rem of Sole sides. ❑❑

Multistyle Winter Hat

Design by Sue Penrod

FINISHED SIZE
One size fits most

MATERIALS

- ❏ Medium (worsted) weight yarn:
  - 3 oz/150 yds/85g each plum and variegated
- ❏ Size K/10½/6.5mm double-ended crochet hook or size needed to obtain gauge
- ❏ Tapestry needle

GAUGE
7 sts = 2 inches 10 rows = 1 inch

PATTERN NOTES
Read General Instructions on pages 3–5 before beginning pattern.

This design is versatile and may be worn as headband, hat or turtleneck.

INSTRUCTIONS

HAT
Row 1: With plum, ch 39, pull up lp in 2nd ch from hook and in each ch

across, turn. *(39 lps on hook)*

Row 2: With variegated, work lps off hook, **do not turn.**

Row 3: Ch 1, sk first vertical bar, pull up lp under both strands of each **horizontal bar** *(see illustration)* across, turn.

Row 4: With plum, work lps off hook, do not turn.

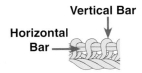

Row 5: Ch 1, skip first vertical bar, pull up lp under both strands of each horizontal bar across, turn.

Rows 6–196: Rep rows 2–5 consecutively, ending with row 4.

Row 197: Ch 1, sl st under both strands of each horizontal bar across. Fasten off.

For seam, sew 22 sts of first and last rows tog.

For drawstring, with variegated, ch 75. Fasten off.

Weave through every other row on unsewn end of Hat.

Pom-pom
Make 2.
Wrap variegated around 2 fingers 36 times, slide lps off fingers, tie separate strand around middle of all lps.

Cut lps, trim. Sew 1 to each end of drawstring.

Pull up drawstring to close top of Hat, tie into bow.

Turn up bottom edge for brim. ❏❏

Butterfly Set

Design by Sandra Miller Maxfield

SKILL LEVEL

INTERMEDIATE

FINISHED SIZES
Place Mat: 12 x 16 inches
Pot Holder: 9 x 9½ inches

MATERIALS

❏ Medium (worsted) weight yarn:
  3½ oz/175 yds/ 99g each purple and pink
  1 oz/50 yds/28g black
❏ Size H/8/5mm crochet hook or size needed to obtain gauge
❏ Size I/9/5.5mm double-ended hook or size needed to obtain gauge
❏ Tapestry needle

GAUGE
Double-ended hook: 7 cls worked in pattern = 4 inches; 11 pattern rows = 2½ inches
Size H hook: 7 sc = 2 inches

PATTERN NOTE
Read General Instructions on pages 3–5 before beginning pattern.

SPECIAL STITCH
Cluster (cl): Yo, pull up lp in top strand of next **horizontal bar** *(see illustration)*, yo, pull through 2 lps on hook, yo, pull up lp in top strand of same horizontal bar, [yo, pull through 2 lps on hook] twice.

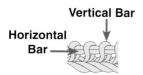

Vertical Bar

Horizontal Bar

INSTRUCTIONS
PLACE MAT
Row 1: With double-ended hook and purple, ch 41, pull up lp in 2nd ch from hook, pull up lp in each ch across, turn. *(41 lps on hook)*
Row 2: With pink, work lps off hook, **do not turn.**
Row 3: Ch 1, [**cl** *(see Special Stitch)* in

top strand of next horizontal bar, pull up lp in top strand of next horizontal bar] across, turn.
Row 4: With purple, work lps off hook, do not turn.
Row 5: Ch 1, [cl in top strand of next horizontal bar, pull up lp in top strand of next horizontal bar] across, turn.
Rows 6–69: Rep rows 2–5 consecutively.
Row 70: With purple, work lps off hook, do not turn.

Edging
Working around outer edge, with size H hook, working around entire horizontal bar, ch 1, 3 sc around first horizontal bar, sc around each horizontal bar across to last horizontal bar, 3 sc around last horizontal bar, evenly sp 34 sc across ends of rows, working in starting ch on opposite side of row 1, 3 sc in first ch, sc in each ch across with 3 sc in last ch, evenly sp 34 sc across ends of rows, join with sl st in beg sc. Fasten off.

POT HOLDER
Wings
Row 1: With double-ended hook and pink, ch 33, pull up lp in 2nd ch from hook, pull up lp in each ch across, turn. *(33 lps on hook)*

Row 2: With purple, work lps off hook, **do not turn.**
Row 3: Ch 1, [cl in top strand of next horizontal bar, pull up lp in top strand of next horizontal bar] across, turn.
Row 4: With pink, work lps off hook, do not turn.
Row 5: Ch 1, [cl in top strand of next horizontal bar, pull up lp in top strand of next horizontal bar] across, turn.
Rows 6–37: Rep rows 2–5 consecutively.
Row 38: With pink, work lps off hook, do not turn.

Edging
Working around outer edge, with size H hook, working around horizontal bar, ch 1, 3 sc around first horizontal bar, sc around each horizontal bar across to last horizontal bar, 3 sc around last horizontal bar, evenly sp 18 sc across ends of rows, working in starting ch on opposite side of row 1, 3 sc in first ch, sc in each ch across with 3 sc in last ch, evenly sp 18 sc across ends of rows, join with sl st in first sc. Fasten off.

Body
With size H hook and black, ch 35, hdc in 3rd ch from hook, hdc in each ch

across with 5 hdc in last ch, working on opposite side of ch, hdc in each ch across, join with sl st in 2nd ch of beg ch-2. Fasten off.

Working vertically, gather across center of Wings to measure 4½ inches. Wrap Body around gathers, sew ends tog, tack in place.

For **hanger**, with size H hook and black, join with sl st in st on top of Body on 1 side, ch 17, sl st in st on other side of Body. Fasten off. ❑❑

Tank Toppers

Design by Sue Penrod

SKILL LEVEL

INTERMEDIATE

FINISHED SIZES
Tissue Cover fits boutique-style tissue box
Toilet Paper Cover fits standard tissue roll

MATERIALS
❑ Medium (worsted) weight yarn:
   4 oz/200 yds/113g each white and blue
❑ Size G/6/4mm double-ended crochet hook or size needed to obtain gauge
❑ 3 nautical ⅝-inch shank buttons
❑ 1 white 1-inch shank button
❑ Tapestry needle

GAUGE
4 sts = 1 inch; 9 rows = 1 inch

PATTERN NOTE
Read General Instructions on pages 3–5 before beginning pattern.

INSTRUCTIONS
TISSUE COVER
Side A
Make 2.
Row 1: With blue, ch 20, pull up lp in 2nd ch from hook, pull up lp in each ch across, turn. *(20 lps on hook)*
Row 2: With white, work lps off hook, **do not turn**.
Row 3: Ch 1, sk first vertical bar, pull up lp in each vertical bar across, turn.
Row 4: With blue, work lps off hook, do not turn.
Row 5: Ch 1, sk first vertical bar, pull up lp in each vertical bar across, turn.
Rows 6–44: Rep rows 2–5 consecutively, ending with row 4.

Row 45: Ch 1, sk first vertical bar, sl st in each vertical bar across. Fasten off.

Side B
Make 1 as written, make 1 reversing colors.
Rows 1–44: Rep same rows of Side A.
Row 45: Ch 1, sk first vertical bar, pull up lp in each vertical bar across, turn.
Row 46: With white, work lps off hook, do not turn.

Row 47: Ch 1, sk first vertical bar, pull up lp in each vertical bar across, turn.
Row 48: For top, with blue, pull through first lp on hook, [yo, pull through 2 lps on hook] across to last 3 lps on hook, for **dec**, yo, pull through last 3 lps on hook, do not turn.
Row 49: Ch 1, sk first vertical bar, pull up lp in each vertical bar across, turn. *(18 lps on hook)*

Row 50: With white, work lps off hook, do not turn.

Row 51: Ch 1, sk first vertical bar, pull up lp in each vertical bar across, turn.

Rows 52–80: Rep rows 48–51 consecutively, ending with row 48 and 2 vertical bars in last row.

Row 81: Ch 1, sk first vertical bar, sl st in last vertical bar. Fasten off.

Sew Sides A and B tog as shown in diagram.

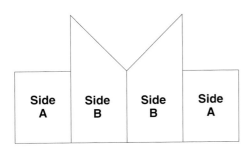

Sew unsewn edges of Sides A on each end tog.

Sew top of each Side A to ends of rows on straight edge of each Side B.

Tack inside corners on angled edge of each Side B tog leaving 3¼ inches unsewn for tissue opening.

Sew 3 small buttons evenly spaced to 1 angled edge.

TOILET TISSUE COVER
Top
Row 1: With blue, ch 7, pull up lp in 2nd ch from hook, pull up lp in each ch across, turn. (*7 lps on hook*)

Row 2: With white, work lps off hook, **do not turn.**

Row 3: Ch 1, sk first vertical bar, pull up lp under each horizontal bar (*see illustration*) across, turn.

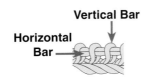

Row 4: With blue, work lps off hook, do not turn.

Row 5: Ch 1, sk first vertical bar, pull up lp under each horizontal bar across, turn.

Rows 6–116: Rep rows 2–5 consecutively, ending with row 4.

Row 117: Ch 1, sk first vertical bar, sl st under each horizontal bar across, **do not turn**, to gather center of Top, ch 1, pull up lp in end of every other row across, yo, pull through all lps on hook, ch 1. Leaving long end for sewing, fasten off.

Sew first and last rows tog.

Side
Row 1: With blue, ch 18, pull up lp in 2nd ch from hook, pull up lp in each ch across, turn. (*18 lps on hook*)

Row 2: With white, work lps off hook, do not turn.

Row 3: Ch 1, sk first vertical bar, pull up lp in each vertical bar across, turn.

Row 4: With blue, work lps off hook, do not turn.

Row 5: Ch 1, sk first vertical bar, pull up lp in each vertical bar across, turn.

Rows 6–116: Rep rows 2–5 consecutively, ending with row 4.

Row 117: Ch 1, sk first vertical bar, sl st in each vertical bar across. Leaving long end for sewing, fasten off.

Sew first and last rows tog.

Sew Top to Side. Sew large button to center of Top. ❏❏

Potpourri Basket

Design by Sue Penrod

SKILL LEVEL

INTERMEDIATE

FINISHED SIZE
4½ inches tall x 5 inches across

MATERIALS
- ❑ Plastic canvas medium (worsted) weight yarn: 2 oz/100 yds/57g each off-white and beige
- ❑ Size H/8/5mm double-ended crochet hook or size needed to obtain gauge
- ❑ Tapestry needle
- ❑ Large wooden bead
- ❑ Thin strip of leather
- ❑ 1 cup *(8 oz.)* round plastic storage container
- ❑ Craft glue or hot-glue gun

GAUGE
4 sts = 1 inch; 12 rows = 1 inch

PATTERN NOTE
Read General Instructions on pages 3–5 before beginning pattern.

INSTRUCTIONS
BASKET
Bottom

Row 1: With beige, ch 9, pull up lp in 2nd ch from hook, pull up lp in each ch across, turn. *(9 lps on hook)*

Row 2: With off-white, work lps off hook, **do not turn.**

Row 3: Ch 1, sk first vertical bar, pull up lp under each **horizontal bar** *(see illustration)* across, turn.

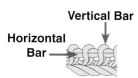

Vertical Bar

Horizontal Bar

Row 4: With beige, work lps off hook, do not turn.

Row 5: Ch 1, sk first vertical bar, pull up lp under each horizontal bar across, turn.

Rows 6–120: Rep rows 2–5 consecutively, ending with row 4.

Row 121: Ch 1, sk first vertical bar, sl st under each horizontal bar across, **do not turn**, to gather bottom of Basket, ch 1, pull up lp in end of every other row across, yo, pull through all lps on hook, ch 1. Leaving long end for sewing, fasten off.
Sew first and last rows tog.

Sides
Row 1: With beige, ch 12, pull up lp in 2nd ch from hook, pull up lp in each ch across, turn. *(12 lps on hook)*

Row 2: With off-white, work lps off hook, **do not turn.**

Row 3: Ch 1, sk first vertical bar, pull up lp under each horizontal bar across, turn.

Row 4: With beige, work lps off hook, do not turn.

Row 5: Ch 1, sk first vertical bar, pull up lp under each horizontal bar across, turn.

Rows 6–180: Rep rows 2–5 consecutively, ending with row 4.

Row 181: Ch 1, sk first vertical bar, sl st under each horizontal bar across. Leaving long end for sewing, fasten off.
Sew first and last rows tog.
Easing to fit, sew Sides and Bottom tog.
Glue plastic container inside Basket Bottom.

Drawstring
With tapestry needle, weave long strand of beige through ends of rows at top of Basket. Pull ends of yarn tight to gather, tie into bow.

LID

Row 1: With beige, ch 6, pull up lp in 2nd ch from hook, pull up lp in each ch across, turn. *(6 lps on hook)*

Row 2: With off-white, work lps off hook, **do not turn.**

Row 3: Ch 1, sk first vertical bar, pull up lp under each horizontal bar across, turn.

Row 4: With beige, work lps off hook, do not turn.

Row 5: Ch 1, sk first vertical bar, pull up lp under each horizontal bar across, turn.

Rows 6–96: Rep rows 2–5 consecutively, ending with row 4.

Row 97: Ch 1, sk first vertical bar, sl st under each horizontal bar across, to gather center of Lid, ch 1, pull up lp in end of every other row across, yo, pull through all lps on hook, ch 1. Leaving long end for sewing, fasten off.

Sew first and last rows tog.

Attach wooden bead to center of Lid with leather strip.

With tapestry needle and off-white, whipstitch around outer edge of Lid.

If desired, with off-white, using chain stitch *(see illustration)*, embroider top of Lid and Basket Sides as shown in photo. ❏❏

Chain Stitch

Microwave Mitt

Design by Debbie Tabor

SKILL LEVEL

INTERMEDIATE

FINISHED SIZE

5 x 7 inches, not including hanging lp

MATERIALS

- ❏ Medium (worsted) weight yarn: 1½ oz/75 yds/43g each dark green and light green ½ oz/25 yds/14g brown
- ❏ Size J/10/6mm double-ended crochet hook or size needed to obtain gauge
- ❏ Tapestry needle
- ❏ Sewing needle
- ❏ 1 spool each of red and white sewing thread
- ❏ 4-inch-square piece red felt

GAUGE

4 sts = 1 inch; 7 rows = 1 inch

PATTERN NOTE

Read General Instructions on pages 3–5 before beginning pattern.

INSTRUCTIONS

MITT

Row 1: With dark green, ch 20, pull up lp in 2nd ch from hook, pull up lp in each ch across, turn. *(20 lps on hook)*

Row 2: With light green, work lps off hook, **do not turn.**

Row 3: Ch 1, sk first vertical bar, pull up lp in top strand of each **horizontal bar** across *(see illustration)*, turn.

Vertical Bar

Horizontal Bar

Row 4: With dark green, work lps off hook, do not turn.

Row 5: Ch 1, sk first vertical bar, pull up lp in top strand of each horizontal bar across, turn.

Rows 6–104: Rep rows 2–5 consecutively, ending with row 4.

Row 105: Ch 1, sk first vertical bar, sl st in top strand of each horizontal bar across. Fasten off.

Hanging Loop

Join dark green with sl st in end of row at center of 1 long edge, ch 12, sl st in same row. Fasten off. Secure ends.

With predominantly light green side of piece facing, fold 4 inches on short ends toward center.

Sew tog at each edge forming pockets. Cut 2 apples from red felt according to pattern.

With sewing thread, sew apple in place on each side.

With brown, using straight stitch (see illustration), embroider 1 stem over each apple.

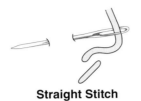

Straight Stitch

With white sewing thread, embroider sparkle accent to 1 corner of each apple as shown in photo. ❏❏

Apple Pattern

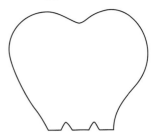

On the Double Floor Protectors

Design by Sue Penrod

SKILL LEVEL

EASY

FINISHED SIZE
3¼ inches tall

MATERIALS FOR FOUR

4 MEDIUM

- ❏ Medium (worsted) weight yarn:
  1½ oz/75 yds/43g each Aran and brown
- ❏ Size G/6/4mm double-ended crochet hook or size needed to obtain gauge
- ❏ Tapestry needle

GAUGE
4 sts = 1 inch; 7 rows = 1 inch

PATTERN NOTE
Read General Instructions on pages 3–5 before beginning pattern.

INSTRUCTIONS
FLOOR PROTECTOR
Make 4.

Row 1: With brown, ch 12, pull up lp in 2nd ch from hook, pull up lp in each ch across, turn. (12 lps on hook)

Row 2: With Aran, work lps off hook, **do not turn.**

Row 3: Sk first vertical bar, pull up lp under each **horizontal bar** across (see illustration), turn.

Vertical Bar

Horizontal Bar →

Row 4: With brown, work lps off hook, do not turn.

Row 5: Sk first vertical bar, pull up lp under each horizontal bar across, turn.

Rows 6–52 or until piece is long enough to fit around chair leg: Rep rows 2–5 consecutively, ending with row 4.

Row 53 or last row: Sk first vertical bar, sl st under each horizontal bar across, **do not turn**, to gather bottom, leaving lps on hook, pull up lp in end of every other row, yo, pull through all lps on hook, ch 1. Leaving long end for sewing, fasten off. Sew first and last rows tog. ❏❏

On the Double Coasters

Design by Sue Penrod

SKILL LEVEL

EASY

FINISHED SIZE

4½ inches across

MATERIALS for 1

- ❏ Medium (worsted) weight yarn: 1 oz/50 yds/28g each of 2 contrasting colors
- ❏ Size G/6/4mm double-ended crochet hook or size needed to obtain gauge
- ❏ Tapestry needle

GAUGE

4 sts = 1 inch; 7 rows = 1 inch

PATTERN NOTE

Read General Instructions on pages 3–5 before beginning pattern.

INSTRUCTIONS

COASTER

Row 1: With first color, ch 8, pull up lp in 2nd ch from hook, pull up lp in each ch across, turn. *(8 lps on hook)*

Row 2: With 2nd color, work lps off hook, **do not turn.**

Row 3: Sk first vertical bar, pull up lp under each **horizontal bar** across *(see illustration)*, turn.

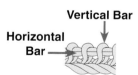

Vertical Bar

Horizontal Bar

Row 4: With first color, work lps off hook, do not turn.

Row 5: Sk first vertical bar, pull up lp under each horizontal bar across, turn.

Rows 6–120: Rep rows 2–5 consecutively, ending with row 4.

Row 121: Sk first vertical bar, sl st under each horizontal bar across, do not turn, leaving lps on hook, pull up lp in end of every other row across, yo, pull through all lps on hook, ch 1. Leaving long end for sewing, fasten off.

Sew first and last rows tog. ❏❏

Christmas Ornaments

Designs by Lori Zeller

WREATH

SKILL LEVEL

INTERMEDIATE

FINISHED SIZE
3 x 3½ inches, not including hanging lp

MATERIALS

- Fine (sport) weight yarn:
  ½ oz/25 yds/14g each dark green and medium green
- Size G/6/4mm double-ended crochet hook or size needed to obtain gauge
- Tapestry needle
- 8 inches green ¹⁄₁₆-inch satin ribbon
- 9 inches red ¼-inch satin picot ribbon
- 3 red 7mm rhinestones
- 1¼ inch white silk poinsettia
- Craft glue or hot-glue gun

GAUGE
11 sts = 2 inches; 7 rows = 1 inch

PATTERN NOTE
Read General Instructions on pages 3–5 before beginning pattern.

INSTRUCTIONS
WREATH
Row 1: With dark green, ch 10, pull up lp in 2nd ch from hook, pull up lp in each ch across, turn. *(10 lps on hook)*

Row 2: With medium green, work lps off hook, **do not turn.**

Row 3: Sk first vertical bar, pull up lp in top strand of each **horizontal bar** across *(see illustration)*, turn.

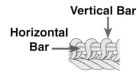

Vertical Bar

Horizontal Bar

Row 4: With dark green, work lps off hook, do not turn.

Row 5: Sk first vertical bar, pull up lp in top strand of each horizontal bar across, turn.

Rows 6–68: Rep rows 2–5 consecutively, ending with row 4. At end of last row, leaving long end for sewing, fasten off.

FINISHING
1. Fold piece in half lengthwise, sew ends of rows tog forming long tube.
2. Sew ends of tube tog.
3. Tie red ribbon into small bow and glue to center bottom of Wreath.
4. Glue poinsettia over red bow.
5. Glue rhinestones to wreath as desired.
6. For **hanging lp**, fold green ribbon in half. Glue ends to top of Wreath on back side.

TREE

SKILL LEVEL

INTERMEDIATE

FINISHED SIZE
3 x 4½ inches, excluding hanging lp

MATERIALS

- Fine (sport) weight yarn:
  ½ oz/25 yds/14g each dark green and medium green
- Size E/4/3.5mm crochet hook
- Size G/6/4mm double-ended crochet hook or size needed to obtain gauge
- 8 inches green ¹⁄₁₆-inch satin ribbon

- ❑ 7 red 7mm rhinestones
- ❑ ½-inch angel charm
- ❑ Craft glue or hot-glue gun

GAUGE

Double-ended hook: 11 sts = 2 inches; 7 rows = 1 inch

PATTERN NOTE

Read General Instructions on pages 3–5 before beginning pattern.

INSTRUCTIONS

TREE
Side
Make 2.

Row 1: With double-ended hook and dark green, ch 2, pull up lp in 2nd ch from hook, turn. *(2 lps on hook)*

Row 2: With medium green, work lps off hook, **do not turn.**

Row 3: Sk first vertical bar, pull up lp in top strand of next **horizontal bar** across *(see illustration)*, pull up lp in last vertical bar, turn. *(3 lps)*

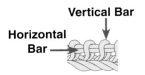

Vertical Bar

Horizontal Bar

Row 4: With dark green, work lps off hook, do not turn.

Row 5: Sk first vertical bar, pull up lp in top strand of each horizontal bar across to last vertical bar, pull up lp in last vertical bar, turn. *(4 lps)*

Row 6: With medium green, work lps off hook, do not turn.

Row 7: Sk first vertical bar, pull up lp in top strand of each horizontal bar across to last vertical bar, pull up lp in last vertical bar, turn. *(5 lps)*

Row 8: With dark green, work lps off hook, do not turn.

Rows 9–32: Rep rows 5–8 consecutively, ending with 17 lps on hook in row 31. At end of last row on first Side, fasten off.

At end of last row on 2nd Side, do not fasten off.

Edging

Holding Sides WS tog, matching sts and working through both thicknesses, with size E hook, ch 1, sk first vertical bar, sc in top strand of next 8 horizontal bars, ch 2, sc in

2nd ch from hook, sc around side of last sc made, sc in top strand of next 8 horizontal bars, ch 2, evenly sp 15 sc across ends of rows, sc in ch on opposite side of row 1, ch 1, sl st in last sc made, sc in same ch, evenly sp 15 sc across ends of rows, ch 2, join with sl st in beg sc. Fasten off.

Glue angel charm to top point of Tree. Glue rhinestones to Tree as desired.

For **hanging lp**, fold green ribbon in half. Glue ends to top of Tree on back side.

DRUMS

SKILL LEVEL

INTERMEDIATE

FINISHED SIZES

Small Drum: 1½ inches tall, excluding hanging lp

Large Drum: 2 inches tall, excluding hanging lp

MATERIALS FOR 1 OF EACH

- ❑ Fine (sport) weight yarn:
    ½ oz/25 yds/14g each green, white and red
- ❑ Size 5 crochet cotton:
    1 yd gold metallic
- ❑ Size D/3/3.25mm crochet hook or size needed to obtain gauge
- ❑ Size G/6/4mm double-ended crochet hook or size needed to obtain gauge
- ❑ Tapestry needle
- ❑ Polyester fiberfill

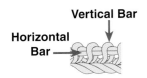

4 MEDIUM

GAUGE

Double-ended hook: 11 sts = 2 inches; 7 rows = 1 inch

Size D hook: Small Drum's Top/Bottom is 1 inch across

PATTERN NOTE

Read General Instructions on pages 3–5 before beginning pattern.

INSTRUCTIONS

SMALL DRUM
Side

Row 1: With double-ended hook and green, ch 8, pull up lp in 2nd ch from hook and in each ch across, turn. *(8 lps on hook)*

Row 2: With red, work lps off hook, **do not turn.**

Row 3: Sk first vertical bar, pull up lp in top strand of each **horizontal bar** across *(see illustration)*, turn.

Vertical Bar

Horizontal Bar

Row 4: With green, work lps off hook, do not turn.

Row 5: Sk first vertical bar, pull up lp in top strand of each horizontal bar across, turn.

Rows 6–28: Rep rows 2–5 consecutively, ending with row 4. At end of last row, leaving long end for sewing, fasten off.

Sew first and last rows tog. Predominantly red side will be outside of Drum.

Top/Bottom
Make 2.

Rnd 1: With size D hook and white, ch 2, 7 sc in 2nd ch from hook, join with sl st in beg sc. *(7 sc)*

Rnd 2: Ch 1, 2 sc in each st around, join with sl st in beg sc. Fasten off.

Sew Top and Bottom pieces to ends of Drum through **back lps** only *(see Stitch Guide)*, stuffing before closing.

With tapestry needle and gold crochet cotton, embroider long zigzag sts around sides of Drum as shown in photo.

For **hanging lp,** tie desired length of gold crochet cotton to st on 1 side of Drum.

LARGE DRUM
Side

Row 1: With double-ended hook and green, ch 11, pull up lp in 2nd ch from hook and in each ch across, turn. *(11 lps on hook)*

Row 2: With red, work lps off hook, **do not turn.**

Row 3: Sk first vertical bar, pull up lp in top strand of each **horizontal bar** across *(see illustration)*, turn.

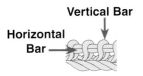

Vertical Bar

Horizontal Bar

Row 4: With green, work lps off hook, do not turn.

Row 5: Sk first vertical bar, pull up lp in top strand of each horizontal bar across, turn.

Rows 6–40: Rep rows 2–5 consecutively, ending with row 4. At end of last row, leaving long end for sewing, fasten off.

Sew first and last rows tog. Predominantly green side will be outside of Drum.

Top/Bottom
Make 2.

Rnds 1 & 2: Rep same rnds of Small Drum's Top/Bottom. At end of last rnd, **do not fasten off.**

Rnd 3: Ch 1, sc in first st, 2 sc in next st, [sc in next st, 2 sc in next st] around, join with sl st in beg sc. Fasten off.

Sew Top and Bottom pieces to ends of Drum through back lps only, stuffing before closing.

With tapestry needle and gold crochet cotton, embroider long zigzag sts around sides of Drum as shown in photo.

For **hanging lp**, tie desired length of gold crochet cotton to st on 1 side of Drum. ❑❑

Cross-Stitch Dishcloth

Design by Jennifer McClain

SKILL LEVEL

INTERMEDIATE

FINISHED SIZE

8 inches square

MATERIALS

- Medium (worsted) weight cotton yarn: 1 oz/50 yds/28g each yellow and variegated
- Size F/5/3.75mm crochet hook or size needed to obtain gauge
- Size G/6/4mm double-ended crochet hook or size needed to obtain gauge

GAUGE

Double-ended hook: 9 sts = 2 inches; 13 pattern rows = 2 inches
Size F hook: 9 sc = 2 inches

PATTERN NOTE

Read General Instructions on pages 3–5 before beginning pattern.

INSTRUCTIONS

Dishcloth

Row 1: With double-ended hook and yellow, ch 35, pull up lp in 2nd ch from hook and in each ch across, turn. *(35 lps on hook)*

Row 2: With variegated, work lps off hook, **do not turn.**

Row 3: Sk first 2 vertical bars, pull up lp in next vertical bar, pull up lp in 2nd sk vertical bar, [sk next

vertical bar, pull up lp in next vertical bar, pull up lp in sk vertical bar] across, turn.

Row 4: With yellow, work lps off hook, do not turn.

Row 5: Sk first vertical bar, pull up lp in next vertical bar, [sk next vertical bar, pull up lp in next vertical bar, pull up lp in sk vertical bar] across to last bar, pull up lp in last bar, turn.

Rows 6–48: Rep rows 2–5 consecutively, ending with row 4.

Row 49: Ch 1, sk first 2 vertical bars,

sl st in next vertical bar, sl st in 2nd sk vertical bar, [sk next vertical bar, sl st in next vertical bar, sl st in sk vertical bar] across. Fasten off.

Edging

With size F hook and yellow, working around outer edge in sts and in ends of rows, join with sc in any corner st, 2 sc in same st, evenly sp sts so piece lies flat, sc around with 3 sc in each corner st, join with sl st in beg sc. Fasten off. ❑❑

Daisy Bath Set

Designs by Bonnie Maxfield

SOAP DISH COVER

SKILL LEVEL
INTERMEDIATE

FINISHED SIZE
Fits standard size soap dish

MATERIALS
- ❏ Medium (worsted) weight yarn: 1 oz/50 yds/28g each #5662 spruce and #5017 natural
- ❏ South Maid size 10 crochet cotton: 50 yds each #1 white, #484 myrtle green and #499 lemon peel
- ❏ Size J/10/6mm double-ended crochet hook or size needed to obtain gauge
- ❏ Size F/5/3.75mm crochet hook
- ❏ Size 5/1.90mm steel crochet hook
- ❏ Tapestry needle

GAUGE
Double-ended hook: 9 sts = 2 inches; 4 pattern rows = 1 inch

PATTERN NOTE
Read General Instructions on pages 3–5 before beginning.

INSTRUCTIONS

COVER
Row 1: With double-ended hook and spruce, ch 11, pull up lp in 2nd ch from hook, pull up lp in each ch across, turn. *(11 lps on hook)*

Row 2: With natural, work lps off hook, **do not turn.**

Row 3: Ch 1, *yo, pull up lp in top strand of next horizontal bar *(see illustration)*, yo, pull though 2 lps on hook, pull up lp in top strand of next horizontal bar, rep from * across, turn.

Vertical Bar

Horizontal Bar

Row 4: With spruce, work lps off hook, do not turn.

Row 5: Ch 1, pull up lp in top strand of each horizontal bar across, turn.

Rows 6–40: Rep rows 2–5 consecutively, ending with row 4 and spruce. Fasten off.

Rnd 41: Working around outer edge in sts and in ends of rows, with size F hook, evenly sp sts so piece lies flat, ch 1, sc around with 3 sc in each corner, join with sl st in beg sc. Fasten off.

With spruce, sew short ends tog through **back lps** *(see Stitch Guide)*.

SMALL DAISY
Rnd 1: With lemon peel and size 5 hook, ch 2, 9 sc in 2nd ch from hook, join with sl st in beg sc. Fasten off. *(9 sc)*

Rnd 2: Join white with sl st in any st, *ch 5, sc in 2nd ch from hook, sc in each ch across**, sl st in next st on rnd 1, rep from * around, ending last rep at **, join with sl st in beg sl st. Fasten off.

Leaf
Make 2.
With myrtle green and size 5 hook, ch 8, sc in 2nd ch from hook, dc in each ch across. Fasten off.
Tack to back of Small Daisy

FINISHING
Tack Small Daisy to Cover as shown in photo.

TISSUE BOX COVER

SKILL LEVEL
INTERMEDIATE

FINISHED SIZE
Fits boutique-style tissue box.

MATERIALS
- ❏ Medium (worsted) weight yarn: 2 oz/100 yds/58g #5662 spruce and #5017 natural
- ❏ Size J/10/6mm double-ended crochet hook or size needed to obtain gauge

- Size F/5/3.75mm
- Tapestry needle

GAUGE
Double-ended hook: 9 sts = 2 inches; 4 pattern rows = 1 inch

PATTERN NOTE
Read General Instructions on pages 3–5 before beginning.

INSTRUCTIONS
COVER
Sides
Row 1: With double-ended hook and spruce, ch 21, pull up lp in 2nd ch from hook, pull up lp in each ch across, turn. (21 lps on hook)

Row 2: With natural, work lps off hook, **do not turn.**

Row 3: Ch 1, *yo, pull up lp in top strand of next **horizontal bar** (see illustration), yo, pull through 2 lps on hook, pull up lp in top strand of next horizontal bar, rep from * across, turn.

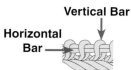

Vertical Bar
Horizontal Bar

Row 4: With spruce, work lps off hook, do not turn.

Row 5: Ch 1, pull up lp in top strand of each horizontal bar across, turn.

Rows 6–76: Rep rows 2–5 consecutively, ending with row 4 and spruce. At end of last row, fasten off.

Rnd 77: Working around outer edge in sts and in ends of rows, with size F hook, evenly sp sts so piece lies flat, ch 1, sc around with 3 sc in each corner, join with sl st in first sc. Fasten off.

With spruce, sew short ends tog through **back lps** (see Stitch Guide).

Top
Make 2.
Rnd 1: With double-ended hook and spruce, ch 17, pull up lp in 2nd ch from hook, pull up lp in each ch across, turn. (17 lps on hook)

Row 2: With soft white, work lps off hook, do not turn.

Row 3: Ch 1, *yo, pull up lp in top strand of next horizontal bar, yo, pull through 2 lps on hook, pull up lp in top strand of next horizontal bar, rep from * across, turn.

Row 4: With spruce, work lps off hook, do not turn.

Row 5: Ch 1, pull up lp in top strand of each horizontal bar across, turn.

Rows 6–8: Rep rows 2–4.

Rnd 9: Working around outer edge in sts and in ends of rows, with size F hook, evenly sp sts so piece lies flat, ch 1, sc around with 3 sc in each corner, join with sl st in first sc. Fasten off.

With spruce, sew short ends tog through **back lps** (see Stitch Guide).

Daisy & Leaf
Work Daisy and Leaf of your choice.

CUP COVER
SKILL LEVEL

INTERMEDIATE

FINISHED SIZE
Fits liquid soap dispenser or cup 2⅝ inches across

MATERIALS

- Medium (worsted) weight yarn:
  1 oz/50 yds/14g #5662 spruce, #5017 natural, #5915 claret and #5690 forest green
- Size J/10/6mm double-end crochet hook or size needed to obtain gauge
- Size F/5/3.75mm crochet hook
- Tapestry needle
- Craft glue or hot-glue gun

GAUGE
Double-ended hook: 9 sts = 2 inches; 4 pattern rows = 1 inch

PATTERN NOTE
Read General Instructions on pages 3–5 before beginning.

INSTRUCTIONS
COVER
Row 1: With double-ended hook and spruce, ch 11, pull up lp in 2nd ch from hook, pull up lp in each ch across, turn. (11 lps on hook)

Row 2: With natural, work lps off hook, do not turn.

Row 3: Ch 1, *yo, pull up lp in top strand of next **horizontal bar** (see illustration), yo, pull through 2 lps on hook, pull up lp in top strand of next horizontal bar, rep from * across, turn.

Vertical Bar
Horizontal Bar

Row 4: With spruce, work lps off hook, do not turn.

Row 5: Ch 1, pull up lp in top strand of each horizontal bar across, turn.

Rows 6–40: Rep rows 2–5 consecutively, ending with row 4 and spruce. At end of last row, fasten off natural.

Rnd 41: Working around outer edge in sts and in ends of rows, with size F hook, evenly sp sts so piece lies flat, ch 1, sc around with 3 sc in each corner, join with sl st in beg sc. Fasten off.

With spruce, sew short ends together through **back lps** (see Stitch Guide).

Daisy & Leaves
Work Daisy and Leaf of your choice.

DAISY
SKILL LEVEL

INTERMEDIATE

FINISHED SIZE
Daises measure from 1½ to 4 inches

MATERIALS
- Medium (worsted) weight yarn:
  1 oz/50 yds/28g each #1 white, #686 paddy green and #230 yellow
- South Maid size 10 crochet cotton: 50 yds each #1 white, #484 myrtle green and #499 lemon peel
- Size 5/1.90mm steel crochet hook or size needed to obtain gauge
- G/6/4mm crochet hook or size needed to obtain gauge
- Tapestry needle

GAUGE
Size G hook and worsted yarn: 4 sc = 1 inch

Size 5 hook and crochet cotton:
8 sc = 1 inch

INSTRUCTIONS

LARGE DAISY

Rnd 1: With yellow and size G hook, ch 2, 11 sc in 2nd ch from hook, join with sl st in first sc. Fasten off. *(11 sc)*

Rnd 2: Join white with sl st in any st, *ch 8, sc in 2nd ch from hook, sc in each ch across**, sl st in next st on rnd 1, rep from * around, ending last rep at **, join with sl st in beg sl st. Fasten off.

Leaf
Make 2.

With paddy green and size G hook, ch 12, sc in 2nd ch from hook, hdc in next ch, dc in each of next 2 chs, tr in each of next 3 chs, dc in each of next 2 chs, hdc in next ch, sc in last ch. Fasten off.
Tack to back of Daisy.

MEDIUM DAISY

Rnd 1: With yellow and size G hook, ch 2, 9 sc in 2nd ch from hook, join with sl st in beg sc. Fasten off. *(9 sc)*

Rnd 2: Join white with sl st in any st, *ch 7, sc in 2nd ch from hook, sc in each ch across**, sl st in next st on rnd 1, rep from * around, ending last rep at **, join with sl st in beg sl st. Fasten off.

Leaf
Make 2.

With paddy green and size G hook, ch 10, sc in 2nd ch from hook, hdc in next ch, dc in each of next 2 chs, tr in each of next 2 chs, dc in next ch, hdc in next ch, sc in last ch. Fasten off. Tack to back of Daisy.

SMALL DAISY

Rnd 1: With lemon peel and size 5 hook, ch 2, 9 sc in 2nd ch from hook, join with sl st in beg sc. Fasten off. *(9 sc)*

Rnd 2: Join white with sl st in any st, *ch 5, sc in 2nd ch from hook, sc in each ch across**, sl st in next st on rnd 1, rep from * around, ending last rep at **, join with sl st in beg sl st. Fasten off.

Leaf
Make 2.

With myrtle green and size 5 hook, ch 8, sc in 2nd ch from hook, dc in each ch across. Fasten off.
Tack to back of Daisy. ❑❑

Daisy Kitchen Set

Designs by Jane Pearson

SKILL LEVEL

INTERMEDIATE

FINISHED SIZES

Dishcloth: 10 x 11½ inches
Towel: 12½ x 17 inches
Dish Soap Bottle Cover:
9½ inches tall

MATERIALS

❑ Medium (worsted) weight cotton yarn: **[4 MEDIUM]**
   3 oz/150 yds/85g each green and variegated
   1 oz/50 yds/28g white
   ½ oz/25 yds/14g yellow
❑ Sizes F/5/3.75mm and G/6/4mm crochet hooks or size needed to obtain gauge
❑ Size H/8/5mm double-ended hook or size needed to obtain gauge
❑ Tapestry needle
❑ Sewing needle
❑ Sewing thread
❑ 18 inches of ¼-inch matching satin ribbon
❑ Desired size button
❑ Crochet stitch markers

GAUGE

Double-ended hook: 3 puff sts and 3 ch sps = 3 inches; 7 rows in pattern = 2 inches

Size G crochet hook: 4 sc = 1 inch; 4 sc rows = 1 inch

PATTERN NOTES

Read General Instructions on pages 3–5 before beginning pattern.

Fasten off colors when no longer needed.

SPECIAL STITCH

Puff stitch (puff st): Pull through 7 lps on hook.

INSTRUCTIONS

DISHCLOTH

Row 1: With double-ended hook and variegated, ch 26, yo, pull up lp in 2nd ch from hook, [yo, pull up lp in next ch] across to last ch, pull up lp in last ch, turn. *(50 lps on hook)*

Row 2: With green, pull through 1 lp on hook, yo, **puff st** *(see special stitches)*, *ch 2, yo, pull through 7 lps on hook *(completes ch-3 and a puff st)*, rep from * across to last 2 lps on hook, ch 1, yo, pull through last 2 lps on hook, **do not turn.**

Row 3: Ch 1, ({yo, pull up lp}, 3 times) in top of each puff st across, pull up lp in last **horizontal bar** *(see illustration)*, turn.

Horizontal Bar

Row 4: With variegated, pull through 1 lp on hook, yo, **puff st** *(see Special Stitch)*, rep from * across to last 2 lps on hook, ch 1, yo, pull through last 2 lps on hook, do not turn.

Row 5: Ch 1, ({yo, pull up lp} 3 times) in top of each puff st across, pull up lp in last horizontal bar, turn.

Rows 6–32: Rep rows 2–5 consecutively, ending with row 4.

Row 33: Ch 2, *({yo, pull up lp} 3 times) in next puff st, yo, pull through all lps on hook, ch 2, rep from * across to last horizontal bar, dc in last horizontal bar. Fasten off.

Edging

Rnd 1: Working around outer edge, with size G hook and green, join with sc in first st, sc in same st, evenly sp 16 sc across to last st, 2 sc in last st, working in ends of rows, evenly sp 25 sc across, working in starting ch on opposite side of row 1, 2 sc in first ch, evenly sp 16 sc across to last ch, 2 sc in last ch, working in ends of row, evenly sp 25 sc across, join with sl st in beg sc. *(90 sc)*

Rnd 2: Ch 1, (sc, ch 2, dc) in first st, sk next st, *(sc, ch 2, dc) in next st, sk next st, rep from * around, join with sl st in beg sc. Fasten off.

TOWEL

Row 1: With double-ended hook and green variegated, ch 35, yo, pull up lp in 2nd ch from hook, [yo, pull up lp in next ch] across to last ch, pull up lp in last ch, turn. *(68 lps on hook)*

Rows 2–36: Rep rows 2–5 of Dishcloth consecutively, ending with row 4.

Top

Row 37: With size G hook, ch 1, sc in first st, evenly sp 23 sc across, turn. *(24 sc)*

Row 38: Ch 1, **sc dec** *(see Stitch Guide)* in first 2 sts, sc in each st across to last 2 sts, sc dec in last 2 sts, turn. *(22 sc)*

Row 39: Ch 1, sc in first st, [sc dec in next 2 sts, sc in next st] across, turn. *(15 sc)*

Row 40: Ch 1, sc dec in first 2 sts, sc in each st across, turn. *(14 sc)*

Rows 41 & 42: Ch 1, sc dec in first 2 sts, sc in each st across to last 2 sts, sc dec in last 2 sts, turn. Ending with 10 sc in last row.

Rows 43–56: Ch 1, sc in each st across, turn.

Row 57: Ch 1, sc dec in first 2 sts, sc in each of next 2 sts, for **buttonhole,** ch 2, sk next 2 sts, sc in each of next 2 sts, sc dec in last 2 sts, turn. *(6 sc, 2 chs)*

Row 58: Ch 1, sc dec in first 2 sts, sc in next st, sc in each of next 2 chs, sc in next st, sc dec in last 2 sts, turn. *(6 sc)*

Rnd 59: Working around outer edge, sc in each of first 6 sts, working in ends of rows, sc in each of next 18 rows, mark last st made, evenly sp 38 sc across, working in starting ch on opposite side of row 1, sc in first ch, evenly sp 33 sc across to last ch, sc in last ch, working in ends of rows, evenly sp 39 sc across ending in row 41, mark last st made, evenly sp 17 sc across, join with sl st in beg sc. Fasten off.

Row 60: With size G hook and green, join with sl st in first marked st, *sk next st, (sc, ch 2, dc) in next st, rep from * 54 times, sk next st, sl st in last marked st. Fasten off. Remove markers.

Sew button in place as shown in photo.

DISH SOAP BOTTLE COVER

Rnd 1: Starting at top, with size G hook and variegated, ch 18, sl st in first ch to form ring, ch 1, sc in first ch, 2 sc in next ch, [sc in next ch, 2 sc in next ch] around, join with sl st in first sc. *(27 sc)*

Rnd 2: Ch 1, sc in each of first 2 sts, 2 sc in next st, [sc in each of next 2 sts, 2 sc in next st] around, join with sl st in beg sc. *(36 sc)*

Rnds 3–6: Ch 1, sc in each st around, join with sl st in beg sc.

Rnd 7: Working this rnd in **back lps** *(see Stitch Guide)*, ch 1, sc in each st around, join with sl st in beg sc.

Rnd 8: Ch 1, sc in each of first 7 sts, sc dec in next 2 sts, [sc in each of next 7 sts, sc dec in next 2 sts] around, join with sl st in beg sc. *(32 sc)*

Rnds 9–12: Ch 1, sc in each st around, join with sl st in beg sc.

Rnd 13: Ch 1, sc in each of first 3 sts, 2 sc in next st, [sc in each of next 3 sts, 2 sc in next st] around, join with sl st in beg sc. *(40 sc)*

Rnds 14–33: Ch 1, sc in each st around, join with sl st in beg sc. At end of last rnd, fasten off.

Bottom Edge

Rnd 34: With size G hook, join white with sc in first st, sc in each st around, join with sl st in beg sc.

Rnd 35: Ch 1, (sc, 2 dc) in first st, ch 1, sk next st, *(sc, 2 dc) in next st, ch 1, sk next st, rep from * around, join with sl st in beg sc. Fasten off.

Top Edging

Rnd 36: With top facing, working in rem lps of rnd 6, with size G hook, join white with sc in first st, 2 sc in next st, [sc in next st, 2 sc in next st] around, join with sl st in beg sc. *(54 sc)*

Rnd 37: Ch 1, (sc, 2 dc) in first st, ch 1, sk next 2 sts, *(sc, 2 dc) in next st, ch 1, sk next 2 sts, rep from * around, join with sl st in beg sc. Fasten off.

Neck Trim

Rnd 38: Working in starting ch on opposite side of rnd 1, with size G hook, join variegated with sc in first ch, sc in each ch around, join with sl st in beg sc. Fasten off.

Flower
Make 3.

Rnd 1: Starting at center, with size F hook and yellow, ch 2, 8 sc in 2nd ch from hook, join with sl st in first sc. Fasten off. *(8 sc)*

Rnd 2: For petals, with size F hook and white, join with sl st in first st, [ch 4, tr, for **picot**, ch 3, sl st in top of last st made, ch 4, sl st) in same st as joining sl st made, (sl st, ch 4, tr, picot, ch 4, sl st) in each st around, join with sl st in beg sl st. Fasten off.

Leaf Spray

With size F hook and green, ch 22, sl st in first ch, ({ch 21, sl st} 2 times) in same ch as last sl st made. Fasten off.

Sew Leaf Spray and Flowers to Cover as shown in photo.

Starting at center front, weave ribbon through sps of rnd 37 on Top Edging. Tie ends. ❏❏

Autumn Place Mat

Design by Eleanor Miles-Bradley

SKILL LEVEL

INTERMEDIATE

FINISHED SIZE
12½ x 18 inches

MATERIALS FOR 1 SET
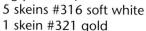

- ❏ Red Heart Super Saver medium (worsted) yarn (7 oz/364 yds/ 198g per skein):
  - 5 skeins #316 soft white
  - 1 skein #321 gold
- ❏ Red Heart Classic medium (worsted) weight yarn (3½ oz/ 198 yds/99g per skein):
  - 1 skein each #334 tan, #336 warm brown, #339 mid brown and #365 coffee
- ❏ Medium (worsted) weight yarn: 3½ oz/198 yds/99g light green
- ❏ Size K/10½/6.5mm double-ended crochet hook or size needed to obtain gauge
- ❏ Size K/10½/6.5mm crochet hook
- ❏ Tapestry needle
- ❏ Fabric glue
- ❏ Paper towels

GAUGE
Double-ended hook: 4 sts = 1 inch; 15 rows = 2 inches

PATTERN NOTE
Read General Instructions on pages 3–5 before beginning pattern.

INSTRUCTIONS
PLACE MAT
Row 1: With double-ended hook and soft white, ch 45, pull up lp in 2nd ch from hook, pull up lp in each ch across, turn. *(45 lps on hook)*

Row 2: With separate skein of soft white, work lps off hook, **do not turn.**

Row 3: Sk first vertical bar, pull up lp in each vertical bar across, turn.

Rows 4–132: Rep rows 2 and 3 alternately, ending with row 2.

Row 133: Sk first vertical bar, sl st in each vertical bar across. Fasten off.

Weaving
Turn crocheted piece so ridges are vertical. Using colors shown on Place Mat Side A Graph, weave yarn through lps across the length of crocheted piece according to graph.

To finish ends, weave yarn back through last 2 lps in the opposite direction, forming lp above the st. Remove needle. Protect work surface to prevent glue damage. Dab a small amount of glue to top of st under the lp, then pull lp tight. *(Use paper towels to clean the tip of the glue bottle frequently.)* When dry, trim yarn close to glue. Rep this process on all ends.

Weave other side of Place Mat according to Side B Graph.

Edging
Working around entire outer edge, with size K hook and soft white, join with sc in first st of last row, ch 2, sc in same st, sc in each st across with (sc, ch 2, sc) in last st, working in ends of rows, sc in each ridge across, working in starting ch on opposite side of row 1, (sc, ch 2, sc) in first ch, sc in each ch across with (sc, ch 2, sc) in last ch, working in ends of rows, sc in each ridge across, join with sl st in beg sc. Fasten off. ❏❏

Side A Graph

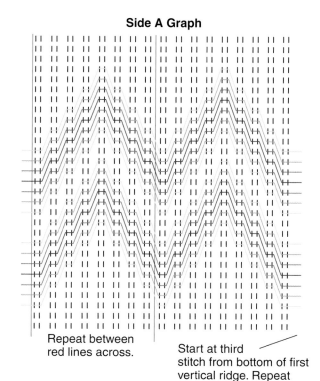

Repeat between red lines across.

Start at third stitch from bottom of first vertical ridge. Repeat line sequence to top of crocheted piece.

Side B Graph

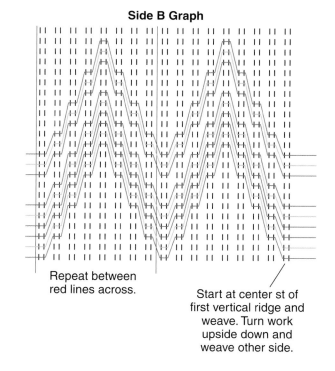

Repeat between red lines across.

Start at center st of first vertical ridge and weave. Turn work upside down and weave other side.

Beautiful Rows Stitch

Design by Ann Parnell

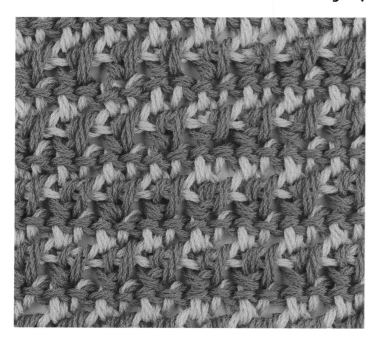

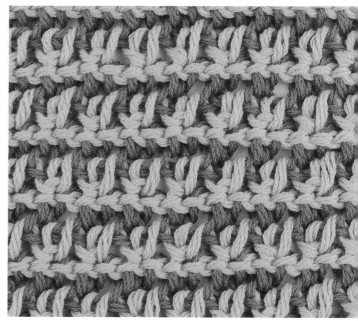

SKILL LEVEL

INTERMEDIATE

MATERIALS
- ❏ Medium (worsted) weight yarn: Amount needed for project each 2 colors (A and B)

MEDIUM

- ❏ Size H/8/5mm double-ended hook used for photographed block

PATTERN NOTE
Read General Instructions on pages 3–5 before beginning pattern.

INSTRUCTIONS

STITCH PATTERN

Row 1: With color A, ch 22 or even number of sts, pull up lp in 2nd ch from hook, pull up lp in each ch across, turn. *(22 lps on hook)*

Row 2: With color B, work lps off hook, **do not turn.**

Row 3: Ch 1, pull up lp in top strand of first **horizontal bar** *(see illustration)*,

Vertical Bar

Horizontal Bar

[yo, sk next horizontal bar, pull up lp in top strand of next horizontal bar] across, turn.

Row 4: With color A, work lps off hook, do not turn.

Row 5: Ch 1, pull up lp in top strand of first horizontal bar, [yo, sk next horizontal bar, pull up lp in top strand of next horizontal bar] across, turn.

Rows 6–28: Rep rows 2–5 consecutively, ending with row 4.

Row 29: Ch 1, sk first vertical bar, sl st in top strand of each horizontal bar across. Fasten off. ❏❏

Knit Bands Stitch

Design by Ann Parnell

SKILL LEVEL

EXPERIENCED

MATERIALS

- ❏ Medium (worsted) weight yarn: Amount needed for project each 2 colors (A and B)
- ❏ Size H/8/5mm double-ended hook used for photographed block

PATTERN NOTE

Read General Instructions on pages 3–5 before beginning pattern.

SPECIAL STITCHES

Knit stitch (k): Insert hook between front and back vertical bars and under **horizontal bar** of next st (see illustration), yo, pull up lp.

Purl stitch (p): Holding yarn in front of work and hook at back of work, insert hook from back to front through back and front vertical bars of next st, yo, pull up lp.

INSTRUCTIONS
STITCH PATTERN

Row 1: With color A, ch 22 or in multiples of 4 plus 2, pull up lp in 2nd ch from hook, pull up lp in each ch across, turn. (22 lps on hook)

Row 2: With color B, work lps off hook, **do not turn.**

Row 3: Sk first vertical bar, **k**1 (see Special Stitches), **p**2 (see Special Stitches), k2, [p2, k2] across, turn.

Row 4: With color A, work lps off hook, do not turn.

Row 5: Sk first vertical bar, p1, [k2, p2] across, turn.

Rows 6–36: Rep rows 2–5 consecutively, ending with row 4.

Row 37: Ch 1, sk first vertical bar, sl st in each vertical bar across. Fasten off. ❏❏

Vertical Bar

Horizontal Bar

Twice as Nice Stitch

Design by Jennifer McClain

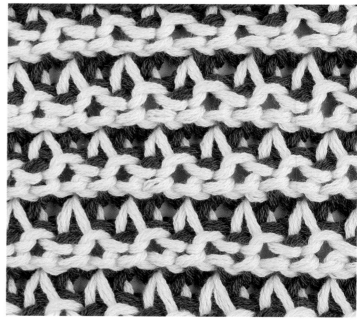

SKILL LEVEL

INTERMEDIATE

MATERIALS
- ❏ Medium (worsted) weight yarn: Amount needed for project each 2 colors (A and B)
- ❏ Size H/8/5mm double-ended hook used for photographed block

MEDIUM 4

PATTERN NOTE
Read General Instructions on pages 3–5 before beginning pattern.

INSTRUCTIONS
STITCH PATTERN
Row 1: With color A, ch 20 or even number of sts, pull up lp in 2nd ch from hook, pull up lp in each ch across, turn. (*20 lps on hook*)

Row 2: With color B, work lps off hook, **do not turn.**

Row 3: Ch 1, *pull up lp in top strand of next **horizontal bar** (*see illustration*), insert hook under next 2 vertical bars at same time, yo, pull up lp, rep from * across to last horizontal bar, pull up lp in top strand of last horizontal bar, turn.

Vertical Bar

Horizontal Bar

Row 4: With color A, work lps off hook, do not turn.

Row 5: Ch 1, *pull up lp in top strand of next horizontal bar, insert hook under next 2 vertical bars at same time, yo, pull up lp, rep from * across to last horizontal bar, pull up lp in top strand of last horizontal bar, turn.

Row 6: With color B, work lps off hook.

Row 7: Ch 1, pull up lp in top strand of each of first 2 horizontal bars, [insert hook under next 2 vertical bars at same time, yo, pull up lp, pull up lp in top strand of next horizontal bar] across to last 2 vertical bars, pull up lp in top strand of last horizontal bar, turn.

Row 8: With color A, work lps off hook, do not turn.

Row 9: Ch 1, pull up lp in top strand of each of first 2 horizontal bars, [insert hook under next 2 vertical bars at same time, yo, pull up lp, pull up lp in top strand of next horizontal bar] across to last 2 vertical bars, pull up lp in top strand of last horizontal bar, turn.

Rows 10–22: Rep rows 2–9 consecutively, ending with row 6 and color B.

Row 23: Ch 1, sl st in top strand of each of next 2 horizontal bars, [sl st in next 2 vertical bars at the same time, sl st in top strand of next horizontal bar] across. Fasten off. ❏❏

Peaks & Valleys Stitch

Design by Jennifer McClain

SKILL LEVEL

INTERMEDIATE

MATERIALS

- ❏ Medium (worsted) weight yarn: Amount needed for project each 2 colors *(A and B)*
- ❏ Size H/8/5mm double-ended hook used for photographed block

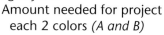

PATTERN NOTE

Read General Instructions on pages 3–5 before beginning pattern.

SPECIAL STITCH

Double crochet loop (dc lp): Yo, insert hook in bar or ch, yo, pull lp through, yo, pull through 2 lps on hook.

INSTRUCTIONS

STITCH PATTERN

Row 1: With color A, ch 21 or in multiples of 3, **dc lp** *(see Special Stitch)* in 3rd ch from hook, dc lp in each ch across, turn. *(20 lps on hook)*

Row 2: With color B, pull through first lp on hook, ch 1, yo, pull through 4 lps on hook *(completes a ch-2 and a shell)* *ch 2, yo, pull through 4 lps on hook *(completes a ch-3 and a shell)*, rep from * across to last 2 lps on hook, ch 1, yo, pull through last 2 lps *(completes a ch-2 and a vertical bar)*, **do not turn.**

Row 3: Ch 1, skipping shells, dc lp in each ch across, turn. *(20 lps on hook)*

Rows 4 & 5: With color A, rep rows 2 and 3.

Rows 6–14: Rep rows 2–5 consecutively, ending with row 2.

Row 15: Ch 2, skipping shells, hdc in each ch across. Fasten off. ❏❏

Horizontal Bar ➞   **Vertical Bar**

Sun & Shadows Stitch

Design by Darla Fanton

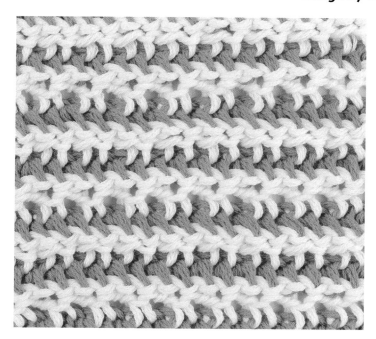

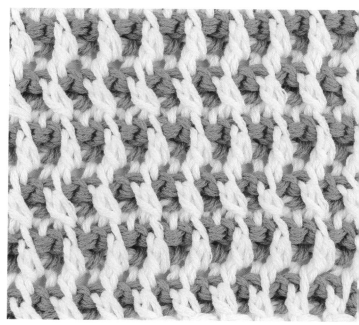

SKILL LEVEL

INTERMEDIATE

MATERIALS

❑ Medium (worsted) weight yarn:
Amount needed for project each 2 colors (A and B)
❑ Size H/8/5mm double-ended hook used for photographed block

(MEDIUM 4 symbol)

PATTERN NOTE

Read General Instructions on pages 3–5 before beginning pattern.

SPECIAL STITCHES

Long half double crochet (lhdc):
Yo, pull up lp in indicated vertical bar 4 rows below, yo, pull lp through, yo, pull through all 3 lps on hook.

Long double crochet (ldc): Yo, pull up lp in vertical bar of next st 4 rows below, yo, pull lp through, yo, pull through 2 lps on hook.

INSTRUCTIONS

STITCH PATTERN

Row 1: With color A, ch 21 or odd number of sts, pull up lp in 2nd ch from hook, pull up lp in each ch across, turn. *(21 lps on hook)*

Row 2: With color B, work lps off hook, **do not turn.**

Row 3: Ch 1, pull up lp in top strand of first **horizontal bar** *(see illustration)*, pull up lp in top strand of each horizontal bar across, turn.

Row 4: With color A, work lps off hook, do not turn.

Row 5: Lhdc *(see Special Stitches)* in first vertical bar 4 rows below, sk first horizontal bar on last row, pull up lp in top strand of next horizontal bar, *sk next vertical bar 4 rows below, **ldc** *(see Special Stitches)* in next vertical bar, sk next horizontal bar on last row, pull up lp in top strand of next horizontal bar, rep from * across to last vertical bar, ldc in last vertical bar 4 rows below, turn.

Vertical Bar

Horizontal Bar

Row 6: With color B, work lps off hook, do not turn.

Row 7: Ch 1, pull up lp in top strand of first horizontal bar, pull up lp in top strand of each horizontal bar across, turn.

Row 8: With color A, work lps off hook, do not turn.

Row 9: Sk first vertical bar 4 rows below, ldc in next vertical bar, sk first horizontal bar of last row, pull up lp in top strand of next horizontal bar, [sk next vertical bar 4 rows below, ldc in next vertical bar, sk next horizontal bar on last row, pull up lp in top strand of next horizontal bar] across, turn.

Rows 10–28: Rep rows 2–9 consecutively, ending with row 4.

Row 29: Lhdc in first vertical bar 4 rows below, sk first horizontal bar on last row, sl st in top strand of next horizontal bar, [sk next vertical bar 4 rows below, lhdc in next vertical bar, sk next horizontal bar on last row, sl st in top strand of next horizontal bar] across to last vertical bar, lhdc in last vertical bar 4 rows below. Fasten off. ❏❏

Pearl Impressions Stitch

Design by Darla Fanton

SKILL LEVEL

INTERMEDIATE

MATERIALS

- ❏ Medium (worsted) weight yarn: Amount needed for project each 2 colors (A and B)
- ❏ Size H/8/5mm double-ended hook used for photographed block

MEDIUM 4

PATTERN NOTE

Read General Instructions on pages 3–5 before beginning pattern.

SPECIAL STITCH

Puff stitch (puff st): Yo, pull up lp in next vertical bar of same color 4 rows below, [yo pull up lp in same bar] twice, yo, pull through 6 lps on hook, ch 1.

INSTRUCTIONS

STITCH PATTERN

Row 1: With color A, ch 23 or in multiples of 8 plus 7, pull up lp in 2nd ch from hook, pull up lp in each ch across, turn. *(23 lps on hook)*

Row 2: With color B, work lps off hook, **do not turn.**

Row 3: Ch 1, pull up lp in top strand of each **horizontal bar** *(see illustration)* across, turn.

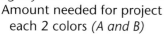

Vertical Bar

Horizontal Bar →

Row 4: With color A, work lps off hook, do not turn.

Row 5: Ch 1, pull up lp in top strand of first 6 horizontal bars, *****puff st** *(see Special Stitch)*, sk next horizontal bar, pull up lp in top strand of next 7 horizontal bars, rep from * across, turn.

Row 6: With color B, work lps off hook, do not turn.

Row 7: Ch 1, pull up lp in top strand of each of first 2 horizontal bars, puff st, sk next horizontal bar, [pull up lp in top strand of each of next 7 horizontal bars, puff st, sk next horizontal bar] across to last 3 horizontal bars, pull up lp in top strand of each of last 3 horizontal bars, turn.

Row 8: With color A, work lps off hook, do not turn.

Row 9: Rep row 7.

Row 10: With color B, work lps off hook, do not turn.

Row 11: Rep row 5.

Rows 12–24: Rep rows 4–11 consecutively, ending with row 8.

Row 25: Ch 1, sl st in top strand of each of first 2 horizontal bars, puff st pulling ch-1 through lp on hook, sk next horizontal bar, [sl st in top strand of each of next 7 horizontal bars, puff st pulling ch-1 through lp on hook, sk next horizontal bar] across to last 3 horizontal bars, sl st in each of last 3 horizontal bars. Fasten off. ❏❏

Knitted Rows Stitch

Design by Ann Parnell

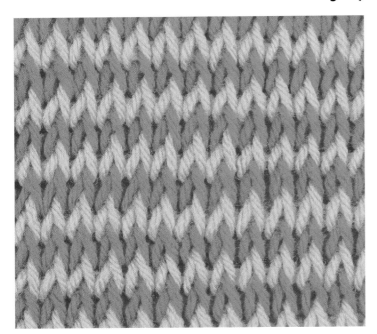

SKILL LEVEL

INTERMEDIATE

MATERIALS
- ❑ Medium (worsted) weight yarn: Amount needed for project each 2 colors *(A and B)*
- ❑ Size K/10½/6.5mm double-ended hook used for photographed block

 4 MEDIUM

PATTERN NOTE
Read General Instructions on pages 3–5 before beginning pattern.

SPECIAL STITCHES
Knit stitch (k) *(see illustration)*: Insert hook between front and back vertical bars and under horizontal bar of next st, yo, pull up lp.

Afghan Knit Stitch

Purl stitch (p): Holding yarn to front of work, and hook at back of work, insert hook from back to front through back and front vertical bars of next st, yo, pull up lp.

INSTRUCTIONS
STITCH PATTERN
Row 1: With color A, ch 20 or desired number of sts, pull up lp in 2nd ch from hook, pull up lp in each ch across, turn. *(20 lps on hook)*

Row 2: With color B, work lps off hook, **do not turn.**

Row 3: Sk first vertical bar, **k** *(see Special Stitches)* across to last vertical bar, for last st, insert hook between first and back vertical bars of last st, yo, pull up lp, turn.

Row 4: With color A, work lps off hook, do not turn.

Row 5: Sk first vertical bar, **p** *(see Special Stitches)* across, turn.

Rows 6–38: Rep rows 2–5 consecutively, ending with row 2.

Row 39: Sl st in each vertical bar across. Fasten off. ❑❑

Vertical Bar

Horizontal Bar

Chevrons Stitch

Design by Dorris Brooks

SKILL LEVEL

INTERMEDIATE

MATERIALS

❑ Medium (worsted) weight yarn:
   Amount needed for project each 2 colors (A and B)
❑ Size K/10½/6.5mm double-ended hook used for photographed block

PATTERN NOTE

Read General Instructions on pages 3–5 before beginning pattern.

SPECIAL STITCH

Long double crochet post stitch (ldc post): Yo, insert hook around both strands of designated vertical bar 4 rows below, yo, pull lp through, yo, pull through 1 lp on hook, yo, pull through 2 lps on hook, yo, pull through 1 lp on hook. Sk horizontal bar on last row behind post stitch.

INSTRUCTIONS

STITCH PATTERN

Row 1: With color A, ch 22 or in multiples of 5 plus 2, pull up lp in 2nd ch from hook, pull up lp in each ch across, turn. *(22 lps on hook)*

Row 2: With color B, work lps off hook, **do not turn.**

Row 3: Ch 1, pull up lp in top strand of each **horizontal bar** *(see illustration)* across, turn.

Row 4: With color A, work lps off hook, do not turn.

Row 5: Ch 1, pull up lp in top strand of each horizontal bar across, turn.

Row 6: With color B, work lps off hook, do not turn.

Row 7: Ldc post *(see Special Stitch)* around 4th vertical bar 4 rows below, pull up lp in top strand of next 3 horizontal bars on last row, *ldc post around same vertical bar 4 rows below, sk next 4 vertical bars 4 rows below, ldc post

Vertical Bar

Horizontal Bar →

around next vertical bar, pull up lp in top strand of next 3 horizontal bars on last row, rep from * across to last 2 horizontal bars on last row, ldc post around same vertical bar 4 rows below, pull up lp in last horizontal bar, turn.

Row 8: With color A, work lps off hook, do not turn.

Row 9: Ch 1, pull up lp in top strand of each horizontal bar across, turn.

Row 10: With color B, work lps off hook, do not turn.

Row 11: Ldc post around vertical bar at center of first post sts 4 rows below, pull up lp in top strand of next 3 horizontal bars on last row, *ldc post around same vertical bar 4 rows below, ldc post around vertical bar at center of next 2 post sts 4 rows below, pull up lp in top strand of next 3 horizontal bars on last row, rep from * across to last 2 horizontal bars on last row, ldc post around same vertical bar 4 rows below, pull up lp in last horizontal bar, turn.

Rows 12–28: Rep rows 8–11 consecutively, ending with row 8.

Row 29: Ch 1, sl st in each horizontal bar across. Fasten off. ❑❑

Post Stitch

Design by Dorris Brooks

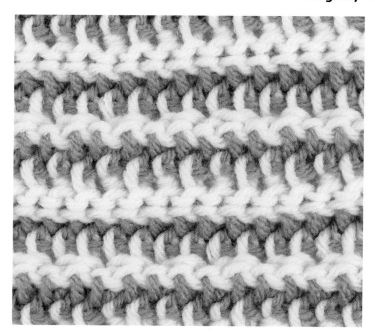

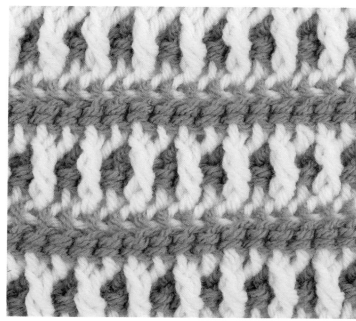

SKILL LEVEL

INTERMEDIATE

MATERIALS

- ❑ Medium (worsted) weight yarn: Amount needed for project each 2 colors (A and B)
- ❑ Size K/10½/6.5mm double-ended hook used for photographed block

MEDIUM

PATTERN NOTE

Read General Instructions on pages 3–5 before beginning pattern.

SPECIAL STITCH

Post stitch (post st): Yo, insert hook around both strands of designated vertical bar 4 rows below, yo, pull lp through 2 lps on hook, ch 1. Sk horizontal bar behind post st on last row.

INSTRUCTIONS
STITCH PATTERN

Row 1: With color A, ch 21 or odd number of sts, pull up lp in 2nd ch from hook, pull up lp in each ch across, turn. *(21 lps on hook)*

Row 2: With color B, work lps off hook, **do not turn.**

Row 3: Ch 1, pull up lp in top strand of each **horizontal bar** *(see illustration)* across, turn.

Vertical Bar

Horizontal Bar →

Row 4: With color A, work lps off hook, do not turn.

Row 5: Ch 1, pull up lp in top strand of each horizontal bar across, turn.

Row 6: With color B, work lps off hook, do not turn.

Row 7: Ch 1, pull up lp in first horizontal bar, ***post st** (see Special Stitch) around 3rd vertical bar 4 rows below, [pull up lp in next horizontal bar on last row, sk next vertical bar 4 rows below, post st around next vertical bar 4 rows below] across to last 2 horizontal bars on last row, pull up lp in last 2 horizontal bars, turn.

Rows 8–24: Rep rows 4–7 consecutively, ending with row 4.

Row 25: Ch 1, sl st in each vertical bar across. Fasten off. ❑❑

Gingham Patch Stitch

Design by Mary Ann Sipes

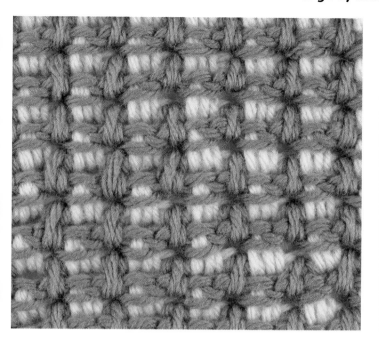
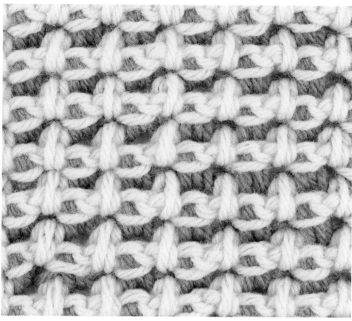

SKILL LEVEL

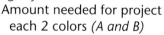

INTERMEDIATE

MATERIALS

❑ Medium (worsted)
weight yarn:
Amount needed for project
each 2 colors *(A and B)*

❑ Size K/10½/6.5mm
double- ended hook used
for photographed block

4
MEDIUM

PATTERN NOTE

Read General Instructions on pages
3–5 before beginning pattern.

INSTRUCTIONS
STITCH PATTERN

Row 1: With color A, ch 16 or even
number of sts, pull up lp in 2nd ch
from hook, yo, pull up lp in same ch,
[sk next ch, pull up lp in next ch, yo,
pull up lp in same ch] across, turn.
(25 lps on hook)

Row 2: With color B, pull through
1 lp on hook, [ch 1, yo, pull
through 4 lps on hook] across, **do
not turn.**

Row 3: Ch 1, [pull up lp in next ch
sp, yo, pull up lp in same ch sp]
across, turn.

Row 4: With color A, pull through 1
lp on hook, [ch 1, yo, pull through 4
lps on hook] across, do not turn.

Row 5: Ch 1, [pull up lp in next ch
sp, yo, pull up lp in same ch sp]
across, turn.

Rows 6–32: Rep rows 2–5 consecutively, ending with row 4. At end of
last row, fasten off. ❑❑

Loop Stitch #1

Design by Dorris Brooks

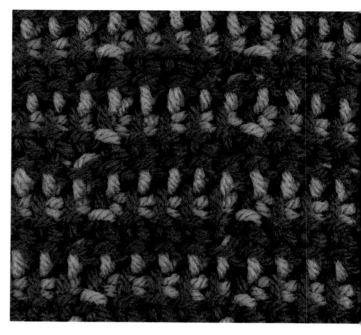

SKILL LEVEL

INTERMEDIATE

MATERIALS

- ❑ Medium (worsted) weight yarn: Amount needed for project each 2 colors *(A and B)*
- ❑ Size K/10½/6.5mm double-ended hook used for photographed block

MEDIUM **4**

PATTERN NOTE

Read General Instructions on pages 3–5 before beginning pattern.

SPECIAL STITCH

Single crochet loop (sc lp): Pull up lp in next bar or st, ch 1.

INSTRUCTIONS
STITCH PATTERN

Row 1: With color A, ch 20 or in multiples of 5, **sc lp** *(see Special Stitch)* in 2nd ch from hook, sc lp in each ch across, turn. *(20 lps on hook)*

Row 2: With color B, pull through first lp on hook, yo, pull through 2 lps on hook, ch 7, *[yo, pull through 2 lps on hook] 5 times, ch 7, rep from * across to last 4 lps on hook, [yo, pull through 2 lps on hook] 3 times, do not turn.

Row 3: Ch 1, sk first vertical bar, pull up lp in each vertical bar across, turn.

Row 4: With A, pull through first lp on hook, [yo, pull through 2 lps on hook] across, do not turn.

Row 5: Ch 1, sk first vertical bar, sc lp in top strand of next **horizontal bar** *(see illustration)*, pull up lp in center ch of next ch lp on 2 rows before last, sk next horizontal bar on last row, [sc lp in top strand of next 4 horizontal bars, pull up lp in center ch of next ch lp on 2 rows before last, sk next horizontal bar on last row] across to last 2 vertical bars, sc lp in top strand of last 2 horizontal bars, turn.

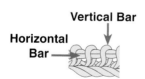

Vertical Bar

Horizontal Bar

Rows 6–24: Rep rows 2–5 consecutively, ending with row 4.

Row 25: Ch 1, sk first vertical bar, sc in top strand of each horizontal bar across. Fasten off. ❑❑

Loop Stitch #2

Design by Dorris Brooks

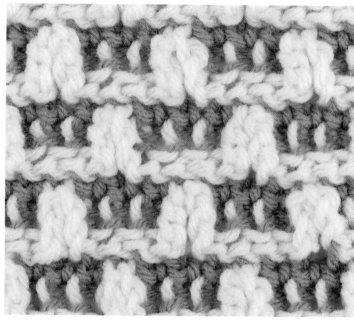

SKILL LEVEL

■■■□

INTERMEDIATE

MATERIALS

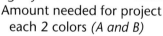

❏ Medium (worsted) weight yarn:
    Amount needed for project each 2 colors (A and B)
❏ Size K/10½/6.5mm double-ended hook used for photographed block

PATTERN NOTE

Read General Instructions on pages 3–5 before beginning pattern.

SPECIAL STITCH

Single crochet loop (sc lp): Pull up lp in next bar or st, ch 1.

INSTRUCTIONS
STITCH PATTERN

Row 1: With color A, ch 21 or in multiples of 4 plus 1, **sc lp** *(see Special Stitch)* in 2nd ch from hook, sc lp in each ch across, turn. *(21 lps on hook)*

Row 2: With B, pull through first lp on hook, yo, pull through 2 lps on hook, ch 6, *[yo, pull through 2 lps on hook] 4 times, ch 6, rep from * 3 times, [yo, pull through 2 lps on hook] 3 times, **do not turn.**

Row 3: Ch 1, sk first vertical bar, skipping ch lps, pull up lp in each vertical bar across, turn.

Row 4: With color A, pull through first lp on hook, [yo, pull through 2 lps on hook] across, do not turn.

Row 5: Ch 1, sk first vertical bar, sc lp in top strand of next horizontal bar, pull up lp in center ch of next ch lp on row before last, sk next horizontal bar on last row, *sc lp in top strand of next 3 horizontal bars, pull up lp in center ch of next ch lp on row before last, sk next horizontal bar on last row, rep from * 3 more times, sc lp in top strand of last 2 horizontal bars, turn.

Vertical Bar

Horizontal Bar

Row 6: With color B, pull through first lp on hook, [yo, pull through 2 lps on hook] 3 times, ch 6, *[yo, pull through 2 lps on hook] 4 times, ch 6, rep from * twice, [yo, pull through 2 lps on hook] 5 times, do not turn.

Row 7: Ch 1, sk first vertical bar, skipping ch lps, pull up lp in each vertical bar across, turn.

Row 8: With color A, pull through first lp on hook, [yo, pull through 2 lps on hook] across, do not turn.

Row 9: Ch 1, sk first vertical bar, *sc lp in top strand of next 3 horizontal bars, pull up lp in center ch of next ch lp on row before last, sk next horizontal bar on last row, rep from * across to last 4 horizontal bars, sc lp in top strand of last 4 horizontal bars, turn.

Rows 10–28: Rep rows 2–9 consecutively, ending with row 4.

Row 29: Ch 1, sk first vertical bar, sc in top strand of each horizontal bar across. Fasten off. ❏❏

Happy Stitch

Design by Darla Fanton

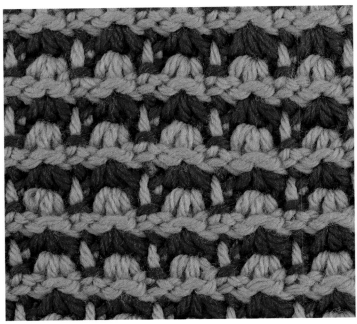

SKILL LEVEL

INTERMEDIATE

MATERIALS

- ❏ Medium (worsted) weight yarn: Amount needed for project each 2 colors (A and B)
- ❏ Size K/10½/6.5mm double-ended hook used for photographed block

MEDIUM

PATTERN NOTE

Read General Instructions on pages 3–5 before beginning pattern.

SPECIAL STITCH

Shell: Yo, pull through 4 lps on hook.

INSTRUCTIONS

STITCH PATTERN

Row 1: With color A, ch 37 or in multiples of 4 plus 1, pull up lp in 2nd ch from hook, pull up lp in each ch across, turn. *(37 lps on hook)*

Row 2: With color B, pull through 1 lp on hook, ***shell** *(see Special Stitch)*, yo, pull through 2 lps on hook, rep from * across, **do not turn.** *(10 lps, 9 shells)*

Row 3: Ch 1, pull up lp in top strand of first **horizontal bar** *(see illustration)*, pull up lp in top of next shell, pull up lp in top strand of next horizontal bar, pull up lp in next vertical bar, *pull up lp in top strand of next horizontal bar, pull up lp in top of next shell, pull up lp in top

strand of next horizontal bar, pull up lp in next vertical bar, rep from * across, turn.

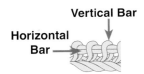

Rows 4 & 5: With color A, rep rows 2 and 3.

Rows 6–36: Rep rows 2–5 consecutively, ending with row 4.

Row 37: Ch 1, [sl st in top strand of next horizontal bar, sl st in next shell, sl st in top strand of next horizontal bar, sl st in next vertical bar] across. Fasten off. ❏❏

Stitch Guide

ABBREVIATIONS

beg	begin/beginning
bpdc	back post double crochet
bpsc	back post single crochet
bptr	back post treble crochet
CC	contrasting color
ch	chain stitch
ch-	refers to chain or space previously made (i.e. ch-1 space)
ch sp	chain space
cl	cluster
cm	centimeter(s)
dc	double crochet
dec	decrease/decreases/decreasing
dtr	double treble crochet
fpdc	front post double crochet
fpsc	front post single crochet
fptr	front post treble crochet
g	gram(s)
hdc	half double crochet
inc	increase/increases/increasing
lp(s)	loop(s)
MC	main color
mm	millimeter(s)
oz	ounce(s)
pc	popcorn
rem	remain/remaining
rep	repeat(s)
rnd(s)	round(s)
RS	right side
sc	single crochet
sk	skip(ped)
sl st	slip stitch
sp(s)	space(s)
st(s)	stitch(es)
tog	together
tr	treble crochet
trtr	triple treble
WS	wrong side
yd(s)	yard(s)
yo	yarn over

Chain—ch: Yo, pull through lp on hook.

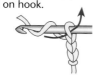

Slip stitch—sl st: Insert hook in st, yo, pull through both lps on hook.

Single crochet—sc: Insert hook in st, yo, pull through st, yo, pull through both lps on hook.

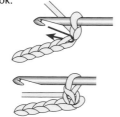

Front loop—front lp Back loop—back lp

Front Loop   Back Loop

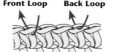

Front post stitch—fp: Back post stitch—bp: When working post st, insert hook from right to left around post st on previous row.

Back   Front

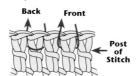

Post of Stitch

Half double crochet—hdc: Yo, insert hook in st, yo, pull through st, yo, pull through all 3 lps on hook.

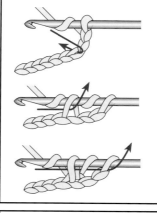

Double crochet—dc: Yo, insert hook in st, yo, pull through st, [yo, pull through 2 lps] twice.

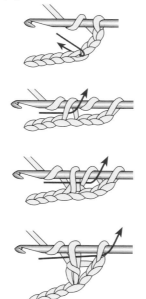

Change colors: Drop first color; with 2nd color, pull through last 2 lps of st.

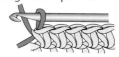

Treble crochet—tr: Yo 2 times, insert hook in st, yo, pull through st, [yo, pull through 2 lps] 3 times.

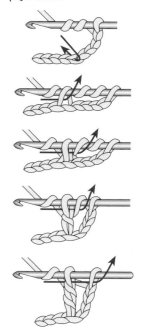

Double treble crochet— dtr: Yo 3 times, insert hook in st, yo, pull through st, [yo, pull through 2 lps] 4 times.

Single crochet decrease (sc dec): (Insert hook, yo, draw up a lp) in each of the sts indicated, yo, draw through all lps on hook.

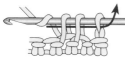

Example of 2-sc dec

Half double crochet decrease (hdc dec): (Yo, insert hook, yo, draw lp through) in each of the sts indicated, yo, draw through all lps on hook.

Example of 2-hdc dec

Double crochet decrease (dc dec): (Yo, insert hook, yo, draw lp through, yo, draw through 2 lps on hook) in each of the sts indicated, yo, draw through all lps on hook.

Example of 2-dc dec

US		UK
sl st (slip stitch)	=	sc (single crochet)
sc (single crochet)	=	dc (double crochet)
hdc (half double crochet)	=	htr (half treble crochet)
dc (double crochet)	=	tr (treble crochet)
tr (treble crochet)	=	dtr (double treble crochet)
dtr (double treble crochet)	=	ttr (triple treble crochet)
skip	=	miss

For more complete information, visit

AnniesAttic.com

ISBN-10: 1-59635-101-2   ISBN-13: 978-1-59635-101-1

Printed in USA   1 2 3 4 5 6 7 8 9